MW01145724

Headphones
and Heartbreaks

A **60-Day Musical Journey** to
Bouncing Back from a **Broken Heart**

By Tikeisha Harris and Janelle Harris Dixon

Headphones
and Heartbreaks

A **60-Day Musical Journey** to
Bouncing Back from a **Broken Heart**

By Tikeisha Harris and Janelle Harris Dixon

Unity Books are available at special discounts for bulk purchases for study groups, book clubs, sales promotions, book signings, or fundraising. To place an order, call the Unity Customer Care Department at 816-251-3571 or email *wholesaleaccts@unityonline.org*.

Cover design: Laura Carl
Interior design: Perfection Press

ISBN: 978-0-87159-429-7
eISBN: 978-0-87159-681-9
Library of Congress Control Number: 2024935869

Dedication

To faith and love ...

and faith in love

Preface

Dear Girlfriends,

At first, we were best friends, comforting and propping each other up as we shared the unfortunate coincidence of having our hearts broken at the same time. Two girls, two exes, two love catastrophes, lots of phone calls and texts flying back and forth between us.

Now it's a blessing to share our intentional journey of healing with you and to create this devotional to help you navigate to the other side of heartbreak. We want to lift other women—even as we have often needed lifting ourselves—which inspired us to write. Along with the support of our mothers, families, friends, and inspirational writing and prayer, we found healing through music.

The title *Headphones and Heartbreaks* is taken from a playlist Janelle saved on her phone after her last breakup, a collection of Beyoncé and Rihanna hits and other songs that made her feel like a warrior when she was doing her afternoon walks and evening workouts. Tikeisha (all of her friends call her "Keisha") came up with the idea for a devotional. When we met for lunch, days into our unceremonious breakups, she said, "Something good has got to come out of this." It did. *Headphones and Heartbreaks* became a thing.

We wrote every part of this book during our individual courses of grief, self-discovery, and communion with God, from the intros when we were freshly bruised to the outros after deep healing. You will journey with us through the raw emotions, perspectives, and revelations we were experiencing and the music we played during the process. We have widely different musical tastes—Keisha is more of a pop enthusiast, Janelle is a patron of soul—but we both enjoy a diversity of inspiration.

We divided up these entries according to emotion so you, as the user, can make the decision to follow the chronological order or navigate the sections based on how you're feeling day-by-day. We also included prayers and activities for you to explore to help vary your journaling and, when you're ready, to usher you back into the fullness of life.

Although we refer to God in the masculine form in our entries, we believe it's a matter of personal choice to identify the Supreme however you choose. We know God as both male and female, Father and Mother, just as strongly as we believe that God is Beginning and End, Alpha and Omega, and we wanted to make note of that for our sisterhood of readers. We've also seen heartbreak flatten people of all genders and identities in roughly the same ways. Feel free to tweak the pronouns and language in these messages to fit your perspective and experience.

To honor the copyright of artists and songwriters, we've quoted song lyrics sparingly. But we invite you to listen to the accompanying *Headphones and Heartbreaks* playlist we created for you at *go.unity.org/ heartbreakplaylist*. It includes all the songs we mention. Read an entry and listen to the related song each day, skip the entry and enjoy just the song, or vice versa. This is an adaptable resource.

Thank you for investing in yourself, and thank you for joining us on this healing journey. If it feels good to you, follow us on Instagram *@th_says* and use our hashtag *#unbroken* to share your bounce-back story. We'd love to celebrate it with you.

With love,

Keisha and *Janelle*

Washington, D.C.
December 31, 2023

Headphones and Heartbreaks Playlist

Hear more than 60 songs that helped Keisha and Janelle bounce back from heartbreak!
go.unity.org/ heartbreakplaylist

SCAN ME

Table of Contents

Keisha's Intro

It was May 2000 the first time I ever felt that ache in my chest. It was the physical pain that resulted from my then-fiancé breaking up with me. I agonizingly understood why people call it *heartbreak*. No relationship since has caused me to emote as much as I did when that one ended, but they all left their own hurt to be processed. The familiar feeling of hope is snatched away when the other person wants out and you still want in. You should be the one in charge of making decisions for your world. But breakups rob you of that sense of control because the person you put your faith in takes over without your permission.

Having been on the wrong side of a breakup more than once, I have learned that I can fall apart and give up altogether on love, or I can rebuild and reframe my life based on what I want next. I refuse to allow someone else to define my world for me. I had no control over their leaving me, but I do have control over my response to their leaving. My choice has been the same each time—I'll cry through it, but I will go on!

I choose to recognize that my time spent loving and giving all of me was not a waste. Instead, I emerge from my heartbreak knowing that a better version of me is coming into existence. The greatest lesson I've learned in heartbreak is that my story is a thread that runs and connects with every other woman who has a story about a time she shared her heart with someone who was not ready to cherish it.

It's that sense of interconnectedness and a bond built with sisters I have never met that inspired the desire to write this devotional. It is a journey of how I found healing through music, inspirational books, friends, my mom, journaling, and prayer.

So I offer this prayer for the sisters who are part of the tapestry of the heartbroken:

God, I don't know who broke their heart, but I know you can heal their pain. I don't know why they were not chosen, but I know *you* are still choosing them.

I know it hurts, and I ask that you give them relief for their pain. I know they feel abandoned and passed over but help them to remember they are still wonderful. God, I pray as they read this, they will feel a step closer to their brighter day!

In Jesus' name,

Amen

Janelle's Intro

You know what's lame? Sitting in the empty café of a 24-hour grocery store at 3 a.m. because your heart is too heavy to be comfortable and your mind is too busy to allow you to sleep through the night. So here I am in a headscarf and raggedy T-shirt, the foulest-looking thing around besides the public bathroom a few feet away.

I didn't love him right away. He's seven years younger than I am and because I didn't have an exemplary success rate with guys in their 20s when I was in my 20s, I paid him no mind when he hit me up on Facebook and suggested we get together. We'd gone to the same college—eons apart, of course—and he contacted me after he'd seen my picture in an alumni group. When he initially inboxed me to flirt, I wouldn't give him my number, but we volleyed messages in casual conversation until he wore me down.

Everything after that was a setup for love. Marathon phone calls that ushered in the sunrise—those long, engrossing discussions that touch on the magnitude of everything and the minutia of nothing important at all. Funny things he said during those conversations made me smile at random as I went through my day and gave me something to look forward to when his number popped up on my phone screen again. We had a lot of those moments.

Before long, there was a first date at IHOP, where he told me I was beautiful and held my hand across the table until our food came. We talked and laughed and played that game where you see who can slap each other's hand the fastest. Four hours flew by and our server teased that we'd been sitting there so long, she thought we were going to fool around and get hungry again. There was another date and another, and more and more hanging out, and pretty soon I was thinking about him all the time.

He told me entirely too late that he didn't want a relationship. He wasn't in a place in his life where he could manage the responsibility of a girlfriend, he said. That was three or four months in, and I was already invested. We kept on dating, me trying to back away from the love I was experiencing, trying to be pretend-casual and pay attention to other dudes so I wouldn't get singularly caught up in the short, stocky, long-lashed chocolate boy who was the frontrunner for my affections. He had told me, in gentle but certain phrases, that it would essentially be foolish for me to do so. I do foolish, though. I do foolish real well.

Everything we did together was so damn fun. Cooking at home and watching TV, exploring the touristy stuff around Washington, D.C., where we live, shooting pool and steadily talking trash, even though neither one of us was especially good at it. Once, we just sat around in my living room and pounded out the beats of old-school R&B songs with our fists in a bootleg game of "Name That Tune." We broke out into *a cappella* versions of Earth, Wind & Fire songs and whittled Stevie Wonder's magnificent catalog down to our two or three absolute favorites. Those moments articulate the simplicity of our joy together. It was easy to fall in love with him and stay there in it.

It wasn't just me, though. I knew he was feeling me something serious when he opted to watch the Super Bowl with me instead of at a sports bar or a party or at home in his own personal space. He did the most thoughtful things on Valentine's Day and my birthday and sometimes just because. He was at my apartment more often than he wasn't. He admitted we were basically a couple. But *basically* isn't. In this context anyway, it was play-play. Pretend. Kinda sorta but not for real. It felt real, though. So I rode that feeling, that risky euphoria, because even if I didn't have the title and the certainty I wanted, I could at least enjoy the experience and live in the moment of being in love.

Sometimes when I'm on the phone with my friends or my mom or my best friend's mom who, bless their hearts, all take turns checking in on me and my feeble pile of emotions, I'll have tears streaming down my cheeks. My heart is crying, even when I'm not. The purge of emotion feels like it's taking forever to complete but in calendar days, it hasn't even been that long.

I wrote these entries from the lived-out pain of two successive heartbreaks that happened unfortunately and staggeringly close together. The men on the opposite side of them are both quality people. I don't take that away from them. But I've been saying, in my effort to recover from first loving and then losing them, that I don't think I can subject myself to being open to falling again.

My friends and family, of course, shush me into silence when I talk like that, but it's only kept me from vocalizing the thought out loud. I've been imposing months of emotional torture on myself, and I keep promising myself that I'll stop and just be open to whatever happens, which is also scary because if I do stay loose and unbothered and still end up living out my days alone, does that mean God destined me to be by myself? Will all of my relationships make a way to get fleeting tastes of what love is but not allow me to indulge in it for my remaining lifetime? That's rough.

I pray for other women in the struggle of not only losing love but making sense of the emotions it forces them to feel. I'm here again too.

Love,

Janelle

ONE
SHOCK

The Crash and Burn

*Let everything happen to you. Beauty and
terror. Just keep going. No feeling is final.*
—Rainer Maria Rilke

The first days are rough. More than likely, you're still in
a state of shock. It's normal to feel numb emotionally.
Since you probably didn't see the breakup coming,
you can't imagine where you go from here. Waking up
with one plan and going to bed with a different reality
is unsettling.

Subconsciously, you may be teetering between
analysis, numbness, and hope, unsure of which space
to land and settle in. Think about it—disasters always
cause panic and confusion initially. Chaos has entered
your world, and you have to give yourself time to process
through it before you can map out a plan to rebuild.

Emotionless, stunned stillness is normal. I didn't cry
in the first days after The Crash and Burn. If you haven't
cried yet, you're not abnormal or broken. Your psyche
has insulated itself so it can process the freight truck
that just hit it. Don't feel like you have to cry or emote
or verbalize in any particular way.

Shock is strange. You're physically present, but your
mind is everywhere and nowhere all at the same time.
You're questioning everything. You're not sure what
you're feeling or what you should feel or how you should
act. It's all a blur, lacking concrete words or ideas.

It's okay. Trust that all of the inner turmoil, the
absence of tears, the questions, the numbness—all of

> **Trust** that all of the inner turmoil, the absence of tears, the questions, the numbness—**all of it is exactly what you need** to be experiencing right at this moment.

it is exactly what you need to be experiencing right at this moment.

Writers and singers create epic songs from their lived-out emotions. They put words and melodies to our thoughts and help us journey deep within to unlock what we need. It's why music serves as a therapeutic conduit for our inner tussling. Rihanna's heartfelt ballad "What Now" sums up shock. (It's on our playlist: *go.unity.org/heartbreakplaylist*.) She describes the emotional place when you don't even know how to feel as your brain tries to understand that you're no longer in the relationship. The lyrics even capture how we initially don't know how to cry. So we find ourselves wrestling with the question, "What am I supposed to do from this point?"

You are the answer to that question. Your *what now?* will emerge as you get up each morning and move about your life. Your *next* didn't depend on your *ex*—you always had the power to create it. That person affected what your next days would look like, but you're in the driver's seat. Define it in small increments, moment by moment, as you heal. Each day will bring its own emotions and its own responses to *what now?* because your feelings, even your numbness, will keep shifting throughout your healing process.—*T.H.*

Affirmation: *I can be at peace in this moment.*

Reflection: Write out what's next for you today. Even if it's as simple as "eat dinner and comfort myself with chocolate cake and cookie dough ice cream," that's your *what now* right now.

God Can Hear Your Heart

I am not promising that God will give you everything you want. There are times when we want things that God knows would not be good for us.—Joyce Meyer

I'm in shock. I need to hear from God because I can't make my mind understand. It's a tangle of thoughts and feelings and memories and nothing is fitting together into any kind of peaceful sense that will let me do anything besides think about me, the man, and this mess.

> Where do I put **this love?**

Where do I put this love? What do I do with this feeling that still lives and breathes on its own inside of me, sometimes wants to grow so big that it almost rips out from my insides? I can't show it, I can't say it, I can't act on it, but pretending doesn't make it not exist. It hurts to want someone so badly and not be wanted as badly back. It hurts even more to feel unheard by God when I plead for answers about it, when all of my prayers are vocalized but seem to go unacknowledged.

It's hard to concentrate on life when your consciousness is consumed by pain. You can't fully focus on anything but how shocked and hurt you are. You probably have a job that demands your undivided attention and competence for stretches of time. You may have children to raise or family members to care for too. But you may only be able to operate at 25, 30, maybe 35 percent because your mind just can't or won't *not* think about it. The breakup.

In one part of "I Need You Now," Smokie Norful pleads with God to come to the rescue right away. That urgency most certainly applies to the sudden trauma of a broken heart. Even if you can't pray big, elaborate prayers, do what you can with short, inarticulate drive-bys, the ones you eke out when you can only manage to string a few words together at a time. The lack of control—of your circumstances, even of your very own emotions—forces you to listen for God because that's all you can do.

Cry to him. Talk to him. Whine to him. Just sit, limp and empty, when you don't have the energy to do anything else. God can hear your heart over your rambling thoughts and failing speech.—*J.H.D.*

>>⫿⫿

Affirmation: *God is always present in my situation.*

Reflection: What about the breakup shocked or surprised you? How have you reacted to it? Do you sense God in the midst of that?

Crazy Mode Loading

Unexpressed emotions will never die. They are buried alive and will come forth later in uglier ways.—Sigmund Freud

I think the first few days of a breakup are probably the worst, when you want to emote what you're feeling to the person who made you feel it. There's a part of you that wants to believe they care and they want to hear your story because you hope they'll see how much they hurt you and will change their minds about the breakup. The other part of you wants to make them suffer with you as you try to make sense of it all.

You might call, you text, you inbox, you email, you show up where you know they'll be to rip them apart, to plead, to cry, to fully give them every emotion you are feeling. I know most people don't put JoJo on their list of top pop singers, but I love her. When she remixed "Marvin's Room (Can't Do Better)," she recaptured my heart again. You can hear the pleas of a woman who calls her ex, hyped on how great she is and questioning how he could ever break up with her.

> The **proud woman** you are so easily crosses over into what men like to call "crazy" mode.

I got it because I've been there and done that and have all the badges to prove it. Something in your brain turns itself off and the proud woman you are so easily crosses over into what men like to call "crazy" mode. They usually use that label to shirk responsibility for their actions, but there's an aspect of truth to how irrational heartbreak can make you. If you were in your most rational state and emotions were not involved, you would probably respond differently. But heartbreaks tend to rip the rational response from most of us.

There's a time and a place for every emotion, as Ecclesiastes 3 reminds. If you don't take the time to acknowledge and process them now, your denial, fear, anger, and pain will come out in other ways later. So take your space now. Lean into your feelings, wrap yourself around them, knowing that even the irrational feelings and responses will pass.—*T.H.*

>▌▌

Affirmation: *I'm not crazy! I'm hurting, I'm in pain, and it's normal to wrestle with my emotions. I will heal and my emotional health will be back at peace.*

Reflection: Step outside of yourself and imagine that you're comforting another woman who is crying and feeling what you're feeling. What advice would you give her in this moment? Does your advice keep her safe? How can you apply the wisdom you're giving to your own healing journey?

The Gift of Grace

*I found peace in the embrace of
God's grace in my immense loss and
overwhelming sadness. Even in those
sad moments, I knew: God was with me,
keeping me ...—Emmanuel Abimbola*

Moping, sadness, and "Why me?" laments are natural by-products of a broken heart. There is a stage where you will fully embrace and live with those emotions and may need to take some time off. But there are also moments where you must still find a voice to praise and serve "In the Middle," as Isaac Carree's song acknowledges.

> Although you're hurting, I really want you to know that **you can still experience God.**

As much as we may want to check out of our lives, it's usually not an option. The Great Breakup happened the night before I had to preach. My sermon was finished, I was ready to get into bed, and hell got loose. I was in total shock on Team No Sleep, but there was no time to call my pastor and switch. I had to preach. There was no out.

Grace is the only reason I could get up the next morning and preach one of my most powerful sermons. Weeks later, I had to pray with a woman experiencing trouble in her relationship, even as my own heart was broken. Again, God's grace met me and I prayed with her rather than grabbing my own tissue and sobbing into it. I still had to facilitate worship services, pray, preach, and teach through heartbreak. God's grace helped me through each moment, strengthening me, giving me peace, keeping me sane, and teaching me more about who God was for me. All of these experiences with grace expanded my love for God.

The heartbreak gave me the chance to walk out what my faith had taught me through the years—that most important is to praise God regardless of my difficulty. Sometimes it was a challenge not to become so upset and angry about my experience that I just let go of God. "In the Middle" reminded me that, in the middle of my tears and confusion, I still intended to celebrate God. I was still willing to accept that Romans 8:28 was true, that God would somehow work this beautiful mess into a greater masterpiece.

Although you're hurting, I really want you to know that you can still experience God. Our faith doesn't make us immune to tears and pain, but it gives you a place to run. It gives you the strength to stand when you don't want to. It gives you the ability to serve and pray for others, even in the middle of your own pain. God's grace will show up just when you need it in the middle of your moments of grief.—*T.H.*

Affirmation: *God's grace is with me, and I have peace because of it.*

Reflection: Journal about a moment when you had to serve or do something for someone else after the breakup and you know God's grace was truly with you. If you're having difficulty praising God right now, reflect on a moment before the breakup when God really blessed you. Use that moment to write a prayer of thanksgiving to God.

TWO
DENIAL

This Can't Be Happening

Denial is a useful defense mechanism until it's not.—Rosalind Kaplan

The moment you realize the other person is saying goodbye, your heart drops. You want to unhear the words. You plead the immortal lyrics of Toni Braxton: "Un-break my heart." Logic and good sense go away and irrationality takes hold. You imagine your ex will wake up and change their mind; they'll call, text, beg, and plead for you to forgive them and go back to how it was right before they said it was over.

> **Don't fight the denial** and don't let other people make you **feel foolish.**

That desire to pretend this is not real is characteristic of denial, an early stage of grief. Loss of love is sad and painful, not unlike the loss from the passing of a loved one. The mind becomes like a turtle, tucking itself away in its shell, too afraid to accept the scariness of a new reality. It's okay to go within. You may even do things you thought you would never do, like beg the person to stay. It's all a part of this stage. Don't beat yourself up. Many have done it before you and many will do it after you.

As the Rosalind Kaplan quote above reminds, denial serves a purpose. Your heart has created a way to cope with a reality that it's not ready to embrace. You will naturally flow from this stage to the next. Don't fight the denial and don't let other people make you feel foolish for holding on to the hope that your world will somehow return to the way it was before your heart was broken. Be true to how you feel until denial no longer serves its purpose to keep you mentally safe.

In time, you will get to the point where you are strong enough to realize there is no way for you to undo what happened. As time passes, you will rebuild your world, and thoughts of the one who said goodbye will become infrequent memories. You will accept that this person is not there and their season in your life has run its course.—*T.H.*

Affirmation: *I don't want to accept that it's over but God, give me strength to believe your truth.*

Reflection: Are you ashamed of yourself for not wanting to let go? What are the secret hopes and thoughts you're holding on to that you're not sharing with anyone else?

Deny, Deny, Deny

Sometimes you need a dose of denial to have hope.—Dr. Kitt Voss, *The Resident*

Before you can truly accept the breakup, there's the stage when you negotiate within yourself that everything will be all right. I remember thinking there was no way he wouldn't be able to see I was "the one." We both felt the energy the moment we met as 16-year-old kids. When we discussed it, he said, "We're always going to be in each other's lives." So my brain had no way to comprehend our not being together anymore. It was not the story either of us wrote.

So many of us have been in a state of denial even before the breakup. Queen Naija's "Lie to Me" lyrics offer a road map to the denial that we live with during a breakup. There can be the denial of seeing problems in the relationship. But even in the breakup, you hit a wall of denial in which you believe they'll be coming back, the relationship was better than it was, or you must change and be a better version of yourself for them to choose you.

> Our psyche needs to slow-walk its way into what our **new reality** will look like.

I had never seen value in denial. It seemed to me that we should all rush to live in our present reality. But the truth is there's a reason why grief has stages. Our psyche needs to slow-walk its way into what our new reality will look like. And it can't get there before it's ready.

I envision our hearts like a baby learning to walk. As much as we can coax and cheer them on, it's still a slow process for their brain and body to align with each other to take a step. Heartbreak is the same. Our brain, our expectations and hopes, and our physical body must catch up to move from denial into hope.

It is in denial that we slow down and catch our breath long enough to keep moving and not unravel. So even if your friends and family think you're foolish to hold out hope that you and your ex will get back together, it's okay to sit for a second and hold this space when you don't want to look at the reality of the moment.

My one piece of advice about this stage is that you don't have to beat up on yourself and you don't have to allow anyone who isn't in your emotional state to dictate how you approach it. Denial may help to soften the hurt, and when it no longer serves you, the emotion will leave.—*T.H.*

Affirmation: *I am where I need to be.*

Reflection: Do you think you are in denial? Are you frustrated with yourself for being in this space? If so, has denial been helpful in your journey?

THREE
QUESTIONING

Was the Love Ever Real?

You can spend minutes, hours, days, weeks, or even months overanalyzing a situation; trying to put the pieces together, justifying what could've, would've happened ... or you can just leave the pieces on the floor and move the f*** on.—Tupac Shakur

You cannot tell me that SZA did not write "I Hate U" for me, because I channel and feel all the feels when I sing it. As she crooned about hate, I would drive around in my car, belting out the lyrics. There are songs that can tap on and allow you to access all the feelings you felt during a breakup, even if it's a decade later. For me, that song will always be one of them.

The lyrics capture the emotional turmoil of heartbreak. The questions. The wonderings. The musings. Then remembering gives way to more questions. *How could he do this to me, to us? Was it real or all a lie? Were those good moments only good for me and not for him?*

> You'll have to just scream at yourself and say, **"*Stop it*. Just stop it."**

Questions rolled around in my brain as I tried to make the implosion of our relationship make sense: *Why? How did I miss it? When will I get over this?* And even more burdensome: *Is this the last time I'll experience love?* Those questions hit hard and can keep you in a chokehold for days. Actually, let's be honest—for months and sometimes years.

Questioning is an inevitable part of breaking up. And if you're analytical like me, the questions can haunt you even more. The most challenging question for me to reconcile was how I could love him and at the same time deeply hate him for breaking my heart. As much as you try to make sense of everything happening to and around you, there's a point when you have to stop trying to unravel it all and use Tupac's statement above as a principle.

You'll have to just scream at yourself and say, "*Stop it. Just stop it.*" This is pointless. I don't have the answers and my ex doesn't either. I've looked at the breakup from every angle and tried to figure out how we ended up here. That's the simplest answer to all of this: We are here. That's all it is. So now I must leave all the questions on the floor and move on.

During my first heartbreak, my moment of moving on came unexpectedly. It was the first time I ever heard God's voice, and it happened while I was listening to Big Pun's "It's So Hard." The voice was so clear, I still remember exactly what it said all these years later: "Get up, wipe your tears, and go read the Psalms."

This phase of questioning is part of your journey, and leaving it behind is way easier said than done. But you will eventually get to the point of both feeling and saying, "Eff it, it's time to move on."—*T.H.*

Affirmation: *I will not overanalyze. Instead, I accept there are new, life-affirming things coming to me now.*

Reflection: What are the most pressing questions you have today? Write them down, get them out of your brain, and leave them on the paper.

QUESTIONING

Put the Devices Down

I am sick at heart. How long, O Lord,
until you restore me?—Psalm 6:3 (NLT)

I woke up in the middle of the night and glanced at the clock. 3:43 a.m. Before I willed myself to go to sleep hours before, I had tucked my phone under a pillow so I'd stop compulsively checking for communication from him. But when I caved and looked at the screen, I swiftly got my feelings hurt. No unread texts. No missed calls. No new emails. Not from him anyway. Wasn't nobody worrying about me but Groupon.

I'm in that phase when you reread and psychoanalyze the texts he sent five days ago because it's the last time you had any contact with him. Yeah, that phase. Frank Ocean's "Thinkin Bout You" is on a mental loop because that's exactly what I'm doing. Too bad I can't make any money off all these thoughts. I could pay cash for a Hummer and flatten out his little forest green Ford Explorer Sport.

> **It's a milestone** every time
> I don't pick up the phone.

I miss him. That's what it really is. I miss him so much that the absence feels heavy, like added body weight. He doesn't deserve to be at the epicenter of my thoughts, so I feel guilty for giving him that much mental real estate, but love keeps him cemented there. I wonder if he's sad too. I wonder if he's already hanging out with other women. I wonder if he's being gut-punched out of his sleep in the middle of the night or if that's an honor that heartache is reserving just for me.

As I get more experience in relationships—not just the romantic ones, but with friends and family as well—I've learned people's personalities aren't easily reduced to all good or all bad. They're complex and intricate and sometimes consequential. He's not a horrible guy. I believe he loved me, just not the way I needed or wanted him to love me. He made reckless decisions with my heart.

We make choices every day based on both our acknowledged emotions and the emotions we want to avoid. I'm lonely, but I don't want to put myself through the regret I'll almost certainly experience afterward if I call him. It's a milestone every time I don't pick up the phone: One hour down and no contact! Six hours! Two days!

There's really nothing either one of us can say anyway except that we miss each other. And that's not a good enough reason to sacrificially struggle along in a relationship that doesn't give me the stability and assurance I need. Right now, I'm just a girl who loved a guy who wasn't "the one," missing him in a big, thought-consuming way but knowing I deserve more than what he's offering.—*J.H.D.*

Affirmation: *Missing him doesn't mean I'm weak or crazy or foolish. It means our relationship meant something real to my heart and that means I'm able to love.*

Reflection: You have a right to speak your heart, and it's your call if you choose to do that directly to the one who has it (for now). Before you contact him, ask yourself three questions:
- Why do I want to talk to him?
- What am I expecting from our conversation?
- How will this help my healing?

Silly in Love

Feelings are never stupid. They just make us feel stupid sometimes.—Laurel K. Hamilton

I don't remember the first time I heard Deniece Williams sing "Silly," but I know I was young. I'm sure I was rocking plaits and singing along with childlike innocence. I missed the pain her words would evoke in women who have loved and lost. Strip away the beauty of her soprano and what's left are the gritty words of a heartbroken woman who wanted to believe she had a good thing.

The lyrics paint a familiar story. Hoping your relationship is "the one"—and ultimately learning it isn't—can leave you feeling silly. The time you spent doting, loving, and supporting your ex can feel as if it was all for nothing.

You feel silly for missing things you did together, silly for missing signs that he was over it, silly that your relationship with God didn't give you some great insight that the breakup was coming and protect you from this heartbreak. You may even feel silly for not listening to the advice of people who warned you about the person who broke your heart.

Rational thinking says it's dumb to keep replaying your relationship and trying to make sense of it all, yet you still find yourself doing just that. You aren't silly, dumb, or any other disparaging adjective that tries to sneak its way into your psyche.

Avoid labeling yourself negatively and recognize that you're feeling the normal side effects of allowing yourself to care, to love, and to give someone room in your sacred space. There is nothing wrong with that. Unfortunately, the other person decided not to fully embrace what you gave, but that doesn't make you silly, even if the hurt you feel tries to tell you otherwise.—*T.H.*

Affirmation: *I'm not silly. I'm not stupid. I was a person who truly loved and will truly love again.*

Reflections: Have you felt stupid? What thoughts triggered that feeling? Do you think you missed something you now wish you hadn't ignored?

Dear God,
I Have Some Questions

There are years that ask questions and years that answer.—Zora Neale Hurston

During the days, weeks, even months that pass after a breakup, there are always lingering questions. In the beginning, your ex may be willing to hear them and try to offer answers. But the answers usually run out before the questions do, and you find yourself still asking even after the person who hurt you has nothing new to reveal.

Then there are the questions you ask your friends in hopes of gaining some greater insight to help it all make sense. Did they see the breakup coming? Did you contribute to it? The questions go on and on until even your friends and family are exhausted.

The greatest answer God gives is the one that helps to assign **meaning to the breakup.**

There are questions you ask yourself. *Could I have done something differently? Was I too demanding? What if I had given in when he asked me to do ___? Would he have stayed?* As elusive as answers may be, something within yearns to make sense of your new reality. Eventually you tire yourself out trying to find answers that, without the other person's input, are only half-truths.

God's not exempt from questions either. They may come in the middle of sobbing uncontrollably or as a last-ditch effort to get answers when you've exhausted all other sources of clarity. Yet The One Who Knows All can be decidedly sovereign and does not always offer insight during the moments we ask. Sometimes God's answer can be silence.

Questioning God reminds me of "Just a Little Talk with Jesus," the song old ladies sang at church when I was young. God will answer eventually in responses that aren't always what we think they should look like. Sometimes there's an unexpected word from someone who reminds you that you're a great person, and sometimes the answer just comes in the comparison of a better relationship. Those *aha* moments help us finish the grieving process.

Personally, I think the greatest answer God gives is the one that helps to assign meaning to the breakup. *What have I learned about myself? What did I learn about what I want?* In identifying the purpose of the breakup and the pain it caused, God's greatest answer emerges and you understand why you went through this experience.—*T.H.*

Affirmation: *I trust God to help me make sense of why I had to go through this experience.*

Reflections: Do you think answers to your questions will make you feel better? How so? What answers from friends, family, or God have been most helpful to assign meaning to the breakup? What clarity have you gotten from within yourself?

Prayer for Mental Quiet

Dear God,

My head is full of thoughts that race around and bounce off each other. I don't have time to make sense out of one before another one piles on top of it and creates a fresh chaos of my mind. I need your peace, not just to calm my scattered emotions but to ease my overactive thinking. When I close my eyes to regroup, let me find you there in quiet communion. Relieve each of my anxieties, release me from the urgency to find answers, and help me regain my focus, my single-mindedness, and my precious, necessary clarity.

In your name,

Amen

FOUR
PAIN

Heartbreak Leave Approved

*Caring for myself is not self-indulgence,
it is self-preservation.*—Audre Lorde

There should be brokenhearted leave. After a breakup, you should be able to file for leave to give yourself a break from work, volunteering, and serving at church. Taking leave would give you permission to lie in bed, sob, listen to sad songs, curl up on the couch, call your girlfriends to talk about how awful he is—all without needing to explain yourself to anyone.

Joking aside, it's important that you make room for yourself in the first stages of getting over heartbreak. More than likely, people won't give you the go-ahead to take a break, to just sit down and catch your breath. Culturally, we don't really allow ourselves and others space to grieve. Western society is constantly rushing forward with to-do lists and ASAP deadlines. So it's not surprising that breakups aren't recognized as high-priority moments that require much-needed healing time.

You are **the only person** who will grant yourself **permission to process** what happened.

You are the only person who will grant yourself permission to process what happened and, in turn, decide where you want to go next. Although we convince ourselves the people who depend on us will not be able to function without us, it's just not true. The world will not stop spinning, sudden disaster will not befall society, and a total collapse of all the things you do won't happen because you take time for yourself.

Don't kid yourself into thinking that God does not grant you the opportunity to take care of yourself. God created the Sabbath to institute the importance of rest. Yet it's often one of the poorest-held practices in our lives. There are moments that force us to stop. Breakups are one of them.

"Getaway," sung so beautifully by Monica, makes it plain that there will be times when we're going to need to escape from the pressures and expectations on us. I love her reminder that everyone at some point needs to get away from the knocks life will throw at you. Although those around you may be expecting you to give more, you have to know when you're at your limit.

Consider your long-term health as opposed to filling short-term requests. It's a detriment to you and even the people you're called to care for if you burn out trying to serve when you really need to rest. Take time to be selfish or self-focused. Care for yourself. Get away. Hide. Rest. Heal.—*T.H.*

Affirmation: *I give myself permission to get away and rest.*

Reflections: Have you given yourself permission to take a break and process your pain? If you haven't, write down who you will call to let them know you'll be out and how long you think you'll need.

PAIN

Unchosen

The human heart doesn't only have so much love to give and we run out. Our love is an endless, renewable resource. We lose love, then find it again.—Paul Carrick Brunson

There may come a time when the men in your life move on. Perhaps even all of your placeholders will get booed up, those in-the-meantime dudes who aren't really boyfriend material but keep you busy until your next real relationship blossoms. Your ex, the one you poured your love into, could turn up with a new girl, or you might learn through a mutual friend that he motored down the matrimonial aisle six months after y'all broke up. Whatever residual pain lingers in your heart may be exacerbated by the sting of being continually unchosen.

I feel left behind, both by him and the life milestones we were supposed to accomplish together. Now he's someone else's boyfriend and I have no doubt they'll get married. That's how it works. You invest and cultivate, the next girl reaps and benefits. It hurts that he gets to be the one to move on first. He's the winner two times over and I'm frustrated with myself for not being over it already. Why am I still affected? Why do I still love him? Why am I not to the point where I can genuinely smile, say congratulations, and mean every syllable of it?

Feelings exhaust me and I wish I could just detach, pull out that part of myself, and be immediately separated from all of the sensitivities and triggers that make me feel overlooked and unworthy. It's a waste of time, energy, and emotion. I imagine him and his new girlfriend in that early-relationship euphoria, laughing together and watching the Philadelphia Eagles play on Sundays. He's probably cooking for her or taking her out to eat when he doesn't feel up to it. I know because those are the things we used to do when we were together.

> You **invest and cultivate,**
> the next girl **reaps and benefits.**

Through all of life's challenges with paying bills and working hard and staying healthy and raising kids or not wanting kids and planning a future and wondering about the present and reflecting on the past, we should have the opportunity to authentically love and be loved. It should be the easiest thing to access and hold on to. In that loveless space, when texts and calls stop coming in, you may feel lonely. Abandoned. Unlovable. Hopeless. But don't. You are not forgotten.

The first lines that André 3000 sings in "Prototype" are a reminder that you're an original model of something that's worth duplicating (but obviously could never be because you're irreplaceable). Even if love fails, your personal greatness need not be called into question.

When your ex finds another partner, it can be tempting to self-compare or reduce yourself to points on a *why-her-and-not-me?* checklist. You are more than a collection of characteristics and traits. You are a force of energy and spirit, and your value isn't based on anyone else's perception, good or bad. It's very possible that you are the answer to someone's prayer or the embodiment of a desire God has for them that they haven't even thought to pray about yet. This is only the end of your love journey if you say it's the end. But if you make the courageous decision to stay open and invite love in, it'll find you again.—*J.H.D.*

≫❪❫

Affirmation: *There will never be anyone like me. I am the prototype.*

Reflections: What qualities make you a good partner? What are your assets and strengths? Are there any areas where you'd like to grow or improve before your next relationship?

Chasing Closure

Some love stories aren't epic novels. Some are short stories. But that doesn't make them any less filled with love.—Carrie Bradshaw, *Sex and the City*

Most of us say or think we need closure after a breakup. I texted for closure. I called for closure. But honestly, I called to reach out and hear his voice. To hope he would change his mind as we got lost in recalling the good moments. That magically, something would happen when he saw my text, and it would rekindle something other than closure.

Then after a while, I really did want closure. Like somehow, a conversation would be the red pill versus the blue pill in *The Matrix*, one that would help me understand and allow me to let go. Or maybe the pill would make all my feelings disappear and I could walk away just like he did.

Closure is accepting that you loved them and your relationship **was special.**

The chase for closure runs the gamut of a breakup. Summer Walker captures the emotions around it in "Closure," a song that details how sometimes looking for finality pulls you into familiar patterns because the love is real. That wasn't our problem. When he was done, he was done. We weren't going on dates, we weren't falling into bed. But the lyrics still resonated with me because chasing closure made me reengage.

Like Summer, I made the mistake too many times of reaching out to him and expecting him to make better sense of what was happening. Instead, I felt myself remembering why I loved him and why I didn't want our relationship to end, even though he wanted it to be done. I had to realize that even as he tried to help me understand, I couldn't. I wasn't ready to break up. Because he was, there was no way our conversations could offer any healing revelations or clarity.

Stop looking for closure, sis. Your ex does not have a magic pill to give you. Closure is accepting that you loved them and your relationship was special—that's why it hurts you to let go and move on. You have to let go because they let go, and only you and the Divine can create true closure. Especially when, more than likely, it's really only confirming the love you have for them, and it's holding you back from closing the book on the relationship.—*T.H.*

Affirmation: *I accept that this love story is over, and I am open to receiving a new love story.*

Reflections: Can you accept that your relationship was love, even though it ended before you were ready? What can you symbolically do to help give yourself closure?

You Don't Have to Be Happy

*Happiness is a deep sense of flourishing ...
not a mere pleasurable feeling, a fleeting
emotion, but an optimal state of being.*
—Matthieu Ricard

I went to bed without crying for two days in a row. I was able to concentrate on tasks for lengthy periods of time, uninterrupted by intrusive memories of him or sorrowful thoughts about his absence. Then I woke up one day without feeling that fluttery ache in my chest and I got excited. *Yay! I think I might be over it!* I silently cheered. *I'm healed! I'm delivered! I think I'm my chipper, happy self again!*

Three hours later, I was sprawled across my sofa with a throw pillow over my face, listening to Jeffrey Osborne. Nobody listens to Jeffrey Osborne under a fresh wind of joy. I was disappointed I'd done such a quick downward spiral. Nothing in particular had even happened to take me back to that point. It snuck up when I wasn't paying attention, just like the unexpected eruption of cheer had that morning.

> We live in a **progress-obsessed culture** that shoves happiness down our gullets.

We live in a progress-obsessed culture that shoves happiness down our gullets. Be happy. Be happy. Be happy, almost to the point where, if you're experiencing any kind of emotional state besides happiness, you may feel like something is tragically wrong with you. We're rushed to get happy through a divorce, through a job loss, through a health crisis when sometimes "happiness" isn't happiness at all. It's often a broad-stroke, generic, filler term for more in-depth concepts like contentment, gratitude, passion, and self-satisfaction.

True, people who identify or socially qualify as happy are markedly healthier than those who don't. A University of Illinois review of more than 160 studies found "clear and compelling evidence" that happier people live longer, are 50 percent less likely to have a stroke or heart attack, and even catch fewer colds than less-happy folks. I mean, those are all compelling reasons to be happy. But other emotions—disappointment, overwhelm, discouragement, frustration, loneliness, fury—are part of the human experience too. No one can be happy all the time. No one *should* be happy all the time.

You attached a hope to someone and they failed you. Miley Cyrus sings in "Flowers" that she can buy her own delights, hold her own hand, and love herself exponentially better than whoever it was who couldn't get it right. You'll be fine too. Be gentle to yourself in the meantime. Get up slowly. Pretending to be happy before you are, to convince yourself or comfort concerned friends and family trying to hurry you back to normal, can be even more stressful than just not being happy.—*J.H.D.*

Affirmation: *I will be happy again. I can be happy again. But I am giving myself time to authentically get there.*

Reflections: Brainstorm a list of 100 things that make you happy. Just the writing of it will lift your spirits.

PAIN

Selective Sharing

I will bless the Lord who guides me; even at night my heart instructs me.—Psalm 16:7 (NLT)

As part of a generation that had Destiny's Child songs to listen to whenever we needed a breakup soundtrack, I play "Girl" in my head when I think about the moments when your girlfriends call an informal meeting to hear what's going on because they just know, without words leaving your lips, that something's wrong.

The dread of having to explain what happened to your friends and family is one of the hardest parts of every breakup. I mentally rehearse how I will efficiently tell the story, and I send up prayers that it will be satisfactory enough that there will be no follow-up questions. But it never happens. There are always more questions.

> Let your family and friends love you, hold you, and encourage you, but **don't leave God out** of the equation.

Once the Q&A is over, the comments meant to cheer you up follow. Someone always offers, "He wasn't good enough for you. You'll find better." They mean well, but when you're grieving, it's the equivalent of a "God knows best" comment after someone you love passes away. Mission fail.

At other times, you're accosted with incredulous questions like "What did you do?" as though the only reason a relationship could end is if you were the guilty party. Honestly, no matter the response, reliving the breakup with someone else feels like a new jab to your already-aching heart.

Friends and family are essential parts of keeping you afloat and preventing you from turning into a disheveled mess but be careful that they're saying what you need to hear. Love is a funny thing: It can prompt people to say and advocate things that are not in line with what God is saying because they want you to feel better. So a loving friend might encourage you to go slash his tires, and another might advise you to call and beg the man to stay—because that's what worked for them.

Let your family and friends love you, hold you, and encourage you, but don't leave God out of the equation. Prayer will help you filter the godly advice from human advice. Speak your truth, tell your story with strength, but listen for God in all of the responses.—*T.H.*

Affirmation: *I have the strength to tell my story. I will discern and embrace good advice.*

Reflections: What's the best advice you've gotten? What's the craziest thing you've heard?
What has God been saying to you as you have been healing? Has it offered you peace?

It Won't Always Hurt This Much

Be soft. Do not let the world make you hard.
Do not let the pain make you hate. Do not
let the bitterness steal your sweetness.
—Iain S. Thomas, *I Wrote This For You*

Someone asked me how I'm doing today and, in the seconds it took them to realize they'd hit a nerve, I threw my hands over my face and let out a little sob. It was ridiculous, bursting out in a cry at what is probably the most basic question one human can inquire about another. Thankfully the storm of emotion came and went fast like summer rain. Freaked out the poor, unsuspecting dude who thought he was just asking a conversational question, though.

I look forward to feeling numb, to allowing my mind and emotions to rest in the ease of blankness. Right now, the city I live in is one big motion of memory. Too many things remind me of him: his favorite movie theater and the restaurant across the street where he ordered wings too spicy for his delicate palate. The new bridge not far from my house that we walked across together, which was cool, except now I think about him every single time I'm near it, on it, or driving by it.

I thought I was past this already, but he still has the ability to hurt me, even in his absence. If I were over it, that wouldn't be the case. I want to be wholly healed and completely free of any feelings for him. He's dangerous to love.

> **Believe something glorious**
> will unfold in the rebuilding
> of your life after this.

Along with the despair and shock, you have a right to be disappointed. The unceremonious end of the relationship is also the unceremonious end of a promise that you believed was going to be yours—to be honored and cherished if you were married, and to be loved and protected if you weren't. The expectations you placed on the relationship didn't happen for the length of time you anticipated, and that is disappointing.

Healing begins with personal choice. Transformation begins with personal choice. I want to get to a place where I can forgive him. God has granted me so much mercy that I want to extend it to someone else. I want to, but I'm not there yet.

Believe something glorious will unfold in the rebuilding of your life after this. Isaiah 43:18–19 (NCV) is a fresh wind of encouragement: "The Lord says, 'Forget what happened before, and do not think about the past. Look at the new thing I am going to do. It is already happening. Don't you see it?'" There will be better, and not necessarily in the form of a better person. A better understanding of yourself. Better empathy for other people. Better compassion and openheartedness in situations that call for it. Better appreciation for love in all forms and the ability to both give it and receive it.

To keep me from deep-diving all the way into crazy, maybe to hold me off from unleashing another random boo-hoo onto an unwitting person, God dropped "After This" by J.J. Hairston into my spirit almost right after The Crash. I looped that joint like it was the soundtrack of life, and honestly, for a while, it was. It played quietly in the back of my mind for weeks for no reason except to let *that* be a reminder too.

There will not only be an "after this"—meaning this is not the end—but there will be glory inside of it. Before God is done with a situation or circumstance, he maximizes it as a learning experience. He is the originator of *"you gon' learn today."* But you'll be wiser, you'll be stronger, and you'll be more prepared to receive and retain what is really yours.—*J.H.D.*

Affirmation: *This is hard, but it will not destroy me. It's making me better.*

Reflections: Write a letter to your ex. What do you want to say? What do you need to get off your chest? Write every thought that comes up. Don't edit your spelling or grammar and don't worry about making sense or being coherent. Let it flow, but don't send the letter when you're done. Throw it away, burn it, or delete it if that helps diffuse the temptation. This is strictly for you. Just purge.

Prayer for Renewal

Dear God,

I want myself back. I want to get back to the me that I was before this heartbreak, freed from the control it has over me but not losing any of the wisdom I gained from the experience. Make me more authentically me than I was before as I embrace a new appreciation of who I am and what I'm worth. Replenish my outward sparkle and my inner joy and restore anything that has been lost in the loss: my faith, my confidence, my loving nature, my trust, my openheartedness, my qualities that make me unique. Help me to move forward without being guarded and cynical. I want to fully and fearlessly be the woman you designed me to be.

In your name,

Amen

FIVE
BARGAINING

Destiny, Not Deal-Making

*The world breaks everyone and afterward
many are strong at the broken places.*
—Ernest Hemingway

In a melancholy rhapsody, Natalie Merchant declares, "I'm Not Gonna Beg." I wish I could say that I was always that adamant and true to myself—to hold my head high and not to beg a boyfriend on his way out the door to still love me and be with me. I wish I could have taken my mom's advice never to beg a man to stay when he's ready to leave. But I have succumbed to wanting to get off the drowning, emotional roller-coaster ride of heartbreak and begged, pleaded, cried, and begged again.

Unfortunately, our pleading and begging isn't limited to another person. You may have found yourself at an altar crying, beside your bed kneeling, or under the covers sobbing for Jesus to fix it. We make promises to do better, go to church more, stop going to the club, and every other thing we think God might be punishing us for, all in hopes that we'll get another chance with our ex.

You may have put aside **your dignity** for a hot second. Grab it back today.

First, I want you to know that you aren't weak. You aren't crazy. You aren't acting "like a girl" or embodying any other demeaning word associations that come with asking the one you love to stay and stop the pain in your heart.

Second, God isn't using this as an opportunity to punish you. He's not requiring you to give up something to change the situation. If you feel like your life is somehow out of step with God, let your conscience guide you to change and grow you into the person God desires you to be. Banish the thought that he is punishing you and that the only way of appeasing him is to strike a bargain in hopes of getting your ex back.

What I do want you to consider is that whatever God has for you is something you don't have to beg for or compromise your beliefs to get. God is not requiring you to grovel, change drastically, or bend over backward to be in a relationship. Trust that if this person is the one for you, God still wants you to be you.

You may have put aside your dignity for a hot second. Grab it back today. Lift your head high and remind yourself of a phrase that my mom would tell me, "What is for you is for you." It is a reminder you can't lose something that is divinely yours. If it was meant for you to be with that person forever, you would be together. You don't have to lose yourself, beg, or plead for someone to love you and choose you. Know that God created you wonderfully fierce and if your ex can't see that, then he wasn't designed for your destiny.—*T.H.*

Affirmation: *I am fierceness walking, and I love every part of me: mind, body, and soul.*

Reflections: Which part(s) of your personhood have you been picking apart as a reason for the breakup? Make a positive, affirming statement for each item you write down. For example, if you write "I wouldn't move in with him," your affirming statement could be "I don't believe in living with a man who's not my husband, and I'm okay with that. The man for me will understand my principles."

Don't Get Back in the Ring

I love you. I hate you. I like you. I hate you. I love you. I think you're stupid. I think you're a loser. I think you're wonderful. I want to be with you. I don't want to be with you. I would never date you. I hate you. I love you ... I think the madness started the moment we met and you shook my hand. Did you have a disease or something?—Shannon L. Alder, The Narcissistic Abuse Recovery Bible

He called. I answered. That was my first mistake. I figured since some time had passed and I'd given myself space to exhale through his absence, I could talk to him and not stumble back into the old familiar habit of adoring him. I'd convinced myself that those feelings were (finally!) fading and it was safe to try to be his friend. So he called and I answered and we laughed and joked like we did pre-breakup, conversation flying between us like everything was normal. It was nice.

Less than 20 minutes later, I was asking him why we weren't together. I was annoyed with myself. That was so not supposed to be in my script.

This is what I know now: I can't be around him and not be in love with him. My common sense knew I wasn't ready to make that huge shift from years-long relationship to platonic friendship, but my subconscious lured me into the lie as a way to talk to him. As if I could just up and demote my feelings. I was disappointed in my willingness to so readily forgive and keep that mushy, sensitive part of myself open, no matter how much I hyped myself up to close it off.

> **I can't be around him** and
> not be in love with him.

Because I stay open, he continues to break my heart and I continue to let him. He rejects me, I get mad, I get over it, I reach out again. That's the ugly, unfortunate cycle. It reminds me of "Holding You Down (Goin' in Circles)" by Jazmine Sullivan: holding him down, getting jerked, coming right back for more. You know how doctors say yo-yo dieting is bad for your heart? So is the repeated start-stop of a relationship that's pleading to be euthanized but keeps getting revived and resuscitated. That emotional masochism is a pain I've imposed on myself.

Now is the time to notice patterns, to pick up on your repeat behaviors and habits so you can analyze them. Pray about and over them. Sit in the reality of them. Journal through them. Heal them. My pattern, I know now, is that I'm never down for the count from one punch. I will come back again and again and again until I'm so emotionally battered or exhausted that I metaphorically can't stand back up.

How many times can someone hurt you? Sometimes, it's as many times as you let them.—*J.H.D.*

Affirmation: *I pay attention to my choices and recommit myself to making the ones that are best for me.*

Reflections: When you look back on your previous relationships, can you notice any behavioral or emotional patterns? What are they? Where do you think they come from?

Productive Bitterness

You're not gonna tell me who I am. I'm gonna tell you who I am.—Nicki Minaj

You know what sucks about having a broken heart besides the actual broken heart itself? Life doesn't stop life-ing while you're immersed in sadness. Your mortgage company doesn't care that you're devastated. The IRS doesn't care. Your acting-up kids don't care. Bill collectors don't care. Your health issues don't care. Your student loans don't care. Your direct supervisor at work most likely doesn't care either.

In the midst of trying to piece yourself back together, the demands and challenges of adulthood are still on full throttle. It ain't like breaking up with your boyfriend of the moment right before sixth period lunch in high school. There are all kinds of needs tugging at your time and attention, fraying your nerves and exacerbating your discouragement. The resulting overwhelm can make you feel like nothing, nothing, nothing is going right.

> My hurt and anger **made me even more driven** to be successful, partly out of spite.

Relationships are a gamble. You're taking a chance that another person will invest in the success of your coupledom with the same intensity, time, and allegiance that you're putting up. Sometimes those levels fluctuate. Sometimes they fail to align altogether. You didn't have a say-so in how long he wanted to stay with you and how hard he loved you, but you can control external factors that comprise other parts of your life.

I don't know if a psychologist would recommend using the bitterness from a broken heart to catalyze achievement, but my hurt and anger made me even more driven to be successful, partly out of spite. I mean, I've always intended to be successful anyway, but it's given me greater incentive to go get my blessings when I imagine myself glammed to the gods to accept an award while he's sitting at home in his funky ball shorts. Or cashing a six-figure check I've earned and rolling past him in a brand-new BMW 750i. (Sometimes in my daydream, it's raining and he gets soaked with puddle water when I drive by.)

My coinciding affirmation, like the Trinidad James' hook in "All Gold Everything," is *Don't believe me? Just watch.* I feel like this right here: If I can't have a storybook love life right now, I'm going to have an amazing career, I'm going to satisfy my wanderlust, and I'm going to have big, plentiful money for me, my daughter, and my mama. Everything outside of that romantic space will absolutely fall into place. There's no other option. The fools who hurt me don't get to win twice. If that's bitterness, let it be productive bitterness.

Checking off accomplishments in more manageable areas can rebuild confidence and remind you of how dope you are. That doesn't have to be a consolation prize for love, but it's a healthy place to focus your energy as you regroup, particularly if your previous life plan was intertwined with his.—*J.H.D.*

Affirmation: *I can and I will be bigger than this grief. I can and I will have what I want. I can and I will become the woman I want to be.*

Reflections: Are you playing small to avoid disappointment? How has this experience made you shrink? How has it inspired you to push yourself into something bigger?

BARGAINING

SIX
ANGER

I'm Just Mad

*A long time ago, I asked God to send me a
decent man. I got Robert, Cedric, Darrell, and
Kenneth. God's got some serious explaining
to do.*—Savannah, *Waiting to Exhale*

"I'm mad all the time. I hate men and their stupid
faces." I sulked and folded my legs into the cushy chair
I favored in my therapist's office. "Is this bitterness?
Am I becoming bitter?"

Dr. Bennett flashed me a small, empathetic smile
from a few feet away. "You're not bitter. You're angry.
What's wrong with letting yourself feel that?"

> He doesn't get to break my
> heart *and* steal my sparkle.

It was overwhelming, the thought of giving myself
permission to be pissed off without a discernible end in
sight. I felt guilty and selfish to park in that space when
I knew so many other people were going through worse
experiences that, in my opinion, genuinely warranted
anger. But I couldn't help how I felt. I put my hands
over my face and blurted a series of raspy sobs. "I don't
want him to win. He doesn't get to break my heart *and*
steal my sparkle. I'm afraid I'm going to stay this way."

Glazing over the fact that Big Sean is a dude and
I'm not feeling his kind, he raps every last one of my

peeved-off feelings in "IDFWU." I am, right now, every stereotype about man-hating, Black woman bitterness. I am Bernadine from *Waiting to Exhale*. I am Pam from *Martin*. I am all of the neck-cocking, teeth-sucking, you-know-men-ain't-no-good-warning aunties who've ever sat around a kitchen table rap session. They're easy to mock until you trace that bitterness back through their personal histories and discover their ferocity is really an expression of unresolved hurt and unfinished grieving. Then it becomes less funny. Then it becomes relatable.

The beautiful part about therapy is *revelation*. It's the worked-for prize. So in that moment, when I was all fragile and vulnerable, my therapist guided me to the realization that I am, to my core, an unrelenting fixer. I don't want to sit in the discomfort of hurt and anger (who does?) and I don't want anyone else to either. So I roll out a standard list of corrective behaviors that blot out the sad or mad. I run to read a post or scripture, say a prayer, listen to music, or call a friend. When those tools don't work their usual magic, I show up to my weekly therapy appointment wanting desperately to experience an *aha* moment that will help me leave feeling more like myself and less like walking despair. In other words, I want her to fix me.

Instead, she tells me that I will come out of my bitter, angry, ugly grief when I am ready. My natural bubbliness will push back to the forefront and I will eventually buoy to normalcy. It won't be prodded or faked or forced. Until then, she says, my homework is to sit in the discomfort of being furious and to be unapologetically okay about it. Maybe that's your homework too.—*J.H.D.*

>>❚❚

Affirmation: *I'm mad and I'm not trying to fix it right now. I'm just mad.*

Reflections: Let's keep it simple. What's your victory for the day?

What Kind of Fool Am I?

Mercy is for people who show remorse.
—Megan Thee Stallion

A unique kind of emotional robbery snatches at your trust when you forgive someone for something they did to wound you, then they consciously do that very same thing again. It's a bold-faced disrespect that takes advantage of your humility and kindness, and it's selfish and ugly and mean.

He cheated and I forgave him. He cheated, I forgave him, and he cheated again.

There is something small and sad about a man who needs to stamp his masculinity by accumulating women. The older that man gets, the more pathetic it becomes, because choosing to amass a personal harem as proof of his virility rather than treating women like valuable human beings with real thoughts and feelings should stop being a goal after puberty has worked its transformational magic. When you've become an adult and racked up some wisdom and good common sense, you should do better because you should know better.

Cheating is the ultimate in betrayals because there's always the option to express unhappiness in the relationship or leave it altogether. Instead, he got greedy. The intentionality behind his decision-making—to text a girl, to put his pants on, to grab his car keys, to sit through red lights, to walk into her house, to do all of his low-down, dirty-dog sex acts, then to stare me dead in my face without a glimmer of visible regret or guilt—is what bothers me the most.

Selflessness is a part of love. You practice self-control for the sake of the other person. He made the deliberate decision to sabotage what we had. Ain't no it-just-happened or I-didn't-think-about-it-that-way.

> A man who can't respect me can't possibly love me the way **I deserve to be loved.**

I wasn't checking for him in the first place. He hit me up. He asked me out. He busted into my life, interrupted my singleness and the comfort I'd built around it, dazzled me with the qualities that made me fall in love, and then he failed me. Ultimately, he let his penis be his primary decision-maker not once, but twice. His insatiable girl-prowling and cavalier excuses—"That's just what guys do," he told me—have created an epic level of doubt in men and myself. I'm pissed. At him, of course, and at myself for forgiving him and giving him the opportunity to play me for a second, even more hurtful time and still loving him in spite of his disregard for me.

Meshell Ndegeocello's "Fool of Me" shuffled onto my playlist yesterday and shoved these pains, regrets, and disappointments to the front of my feelings. Made even more famous in the play-for-your-heart scene in *Love & Basketball*, it's now one of the many songs that articulate my hurt and fury, especially when Meshell

ANGER

agonizes that someone she once desired made her feel dumb and set aside too.

A man who can't respect me can't possibly love me the way I deserve to be loved. That song is an anthem for him because he did in fact make a fool of me, but it also reminded me that I'm exquisitely capable of learning from decisions I wish I could do over to make myself better.—*J.H.D.*

Affirmation: *I am becoming more powerful, more confident, more myself every day.*

Reflections: Has trusting God been a challenge for you? What have you learned in this turbulent moment that makes you more trusting of both God and yourself?

God Created Anger

Go ahead and be angry. You do well to be angry—but don't use your anger as fuel for revenge. And don't stay angry. Don't go to bed angry. Don't give the Devil that kind of foothold in your life.—Ephesians 4:26-27 (MSG)

Christian culture often tries to shame believers and others from feeling anger. Fact: Anger is an emotion and, like love, it is God-created. Search the Bible and we find many instances of God's anger, so it shouldn't surprise us that part of the grieving process is anger for being wronged. Anger will come and go. Let it.

Anger will come and go. Let it.

Jazmine Sullivan's "Bust Your Windows" captured how "get-back" is a part of the heartbreak journey. The heart tries to transfer some of its pain to the person who caused your world to crumble. Your anger might produce creative ideas like busting out car windows, pouring sugar into gas tanks, or putting baby oil on his steps (that's my own creative idea) in the hopes that it will dish out a just punishment and make you feel better. But we're too afraid to let the "saints" know our thoughts of revenge for fear they'll label us with a scarlet letter denoting us as bad Christians.

ANGER

Don't believe it. You're not a bad person—you're a real person. Let the thoughts come and go. Some days you'll find yourself wishing and even wanting to enact a just punishment. It's natural but take the biblical warning this way: Don't become so obsessed with your anger and feed it so much that you find yourself moving from thinking to doing, which is where the danger lies. I know your ex hurt you, but it's not worth catching a case over.

Instead, embrace the reminder in Romans 12:19 to leave room for the situation to be handled by God, who has the ability to avenge any wrong done to you. He knows all and judges the heart of the other person(s) involved, so let God fight your battle.—*T.H.*

Affirmation: *I am not a bad person for being angry, but I will not allow anger to consume me. Instead, I trust God to fight my battles.*

Reflections: Do you feel bad for feeling angry? If so, why? Has your anger gone past healthy and started heading toward dangerous?

He's Already Moved On

You big, dumb, dummy head.—Angie,
Shark Tale

He has a new girlfriend. He has a *new* girlfriend. He has a new *girlfriend.*

It came out as a backfired joke. We had talked infrequently since the breakup but in an attempt to be friends—or just friendly, at the very least—I teased him about being afraid to hang out with me because he would get in trouble with his woman. He asked me how I knew about her.

It was a subtle flirt gone sickeningly wrong. If it could ever be physiologically possible for the human heart to spontaneously tear, mine did, one part rocketing up into my throat so hard that it forced tears over my water line, the other dropping like a brick into my stomach and making me physically queasy.

He doesn't want me. It's really, *really* real. I don't have to guess or wonder. He came out and told me as much. It won't work, he said, then confirmed it by getting on with life accompanied by someone else. I can't dislike her because I don't know her but she's darn sure benefiting from my outpouring of encouragement, support, and love for him. My cheerleading, suggestions, and sacrifice. My let-me-show-you-how-to-do-this and sure-babe-I-can-help-you-do-that. I renovated the man she's now claiming.

ANGER

I loved him strong and made compassionate space for his assorted quirks, flaws, shortcomings, and hangups. Now he gets to move on first? I'm still being overwhelmed with emotion and choking on tears at the most random times, and he's moved so far past it that he's able to rebound already?

> **No more build-a-man projects,** I swear.

May every barber who tries to line his shape-up come down with a bad case of the shakes.

May the DJ evermore cut off his favorite song just when it's getting to his favorite part.

May birds with butts full of the blackest berry juice be waiting for him after he leaves the car wash.

May he come down with a coughing fit whenever he's walking through a cluster of gnats.

May he get popcorn stuck in his teeth whenever he eats it and never once be close to floss or a toothpick.

In the process of cursing him for his ability to get over me so quickly and merge seamlessly back into dating, I've been praying for a pill, a chant, an unlove potion, anything to instantaneously purge me of my emotional wooziness over him. That isn't real, but this epiphany is: No more build-a-man projects, I swear. I vow if a dude doesn't know how to do something or doesn't already possess a quality when he meets me, I will not help him master it for the benefit of the next woman. Until then, I've got the angriest of all ex-girlfriend anthems—Alanis Morissette's "You Oughta Know"—on repeat because not only should he know better, but I hope he keeps finding out what he gave up when he lost me.—*J.H.D.*

Affirmation: *I'm in the business of making myself better.*

Reflections: Has your ex moved on already? How does that make you feel? How are you redirecting that emotion?

Wrestling with God

The Christian does not think God will love us because we are good, but that God will make us good because he loves us.—C.S. Lewis

What happens when what we think we hear God say doesn't align with what actually unfolds in our lives? Luke 1:37 reads a number of ways, depending on the translation, but the sentiment is consistent:

Nothing is impossible for God! (CEV)
There is nothing that God cannot do. (GNT)
God can do anything! (NCV)
For with God nothing will be impossible.
(NKJV)
For every promise from God shall surely come true. (TLB)

And yet, God didn't do *this* thing you wanted.

There can be anxiety around not knowing what will happen in the future. But there's added anxiety around knowing God can make anything come to pass, yet despite your expecting something great and praying with anticipation, maybe even hearing whispers of confirmation from the Holy Spirit, the desires of your heart have not manifested. You're still single. You're recently divorced. You're brokenhearted. It can cause brokenness in both the earthly realm and in the spiritual because you're not only disappointed in man, you're disappointed in God.

In the first few days after The Crash, I would wake up hearing Al Green croon "How Can You Mend a Broken Heart" in the back of my mind, as if I were watching myself act out a dramatic movie scene. The man I loved had killed my insides, but the heartbreak was twofold because I felt like God had let me fall into yet another heartbreak unprotected. The question wasn't just how can I mend my broken heart but how many broken hearts can one woman take?

> Sometimes it seems like God has **broken your heart** too.

I'm wrestling with God. I mean, really wrestling. I've been praying. I've been waiting. I've been anticipating and expecting. I'm discouraged and frustrated and I need answers from the only one who has them. If I'm supposed to be granted the desires of my heart and God is in fact capable of doing all things, when will the fruit of my faith show up?

Sometimes it seems like God has broken your heart too. But—here's the mind pretzel—in order to heal, you have to express those hurt feelings, those unmet expectations, those unfulfilled hopes to God so he can deliver you from them and remedy your crisis of faith. You may never get a this-is-why explanation. That's hard. You just have to trust that the reason it didn't work the way you were praying it would is divine intervention. That's hard too.—*J.H.D.*

Affirmation: *I'm free to tell God when I'm angry with him. He can handle it.*

Reflections: Is it difficult to see God's presence in this situation? In what areas is he missing in action? How does that make you feel? How have you handled it? Make a short video talking strictly to God to vent your raw feelings.

Smite My Enemies

Until you do right by me, everything you think about is gonna crumble.—Miss Celie, *The Color Purple*

This is gonna sound real unholy. Super Christians cover thine eyes.

I want God to avenge my hurt. I want him to make that man feel my absence in his bone marrow, to wrestle him down into the biggest *aha* moment of his whole fool life and force him to pay attention to the empty space that now exists where I used to be.

May the creative hand of divine justice deal him **good ol' fashioned get-back.**

I want him to regret the trade-off he made, the destruction of our relationship and the apparent happiness we shared. I want him to recognize the damage he has inflicted on someone who loved him wholly and authentically—flaws and all. I want him to confess the mistakes he consistently glazes over in his remixed telling of our story.

I want him to feel troubled about the way our love ended—can't sleep, don't want to hang out, not his normal self troubled. I want every new attempt to rebound or fill my spot to be a failure. I want him to

ANGER

87

struggle for a while. And I want him to be fully aware that this is all because of the way he treated me. I want it to have some "this is for Janelle!" sting to it. Breaking my heart was the result of conscious choices he made, which essentially means breaking my heart was a conscious choice. It only seems fair.

Of all the revenge songs, Mariah Carey's "Someday" is a personal anthem for any woman who has ever been dissed by a guy. It's a seemingly innocent up-tempo pop hit but inside those lyrics are the sentiments of a girl who envisions herself glowing up to screw it to the dude who screwed it to her. You may not want to see him maimed or homeless (or maybe you do, I don't know), but you just want him to be fully aware that he was a jerk, be genuinely sorry for it, and never willfully hurt another woman who gives her love to him.

Someday you'll be fully recovered and not even thinking about him, but may the creative hand of divine justice deal him good ol' fashioned get-back with your name all over it even when you're not.—*J.H.D.*

Affirmation: *God is positioning and preparing me to bounce back even better than I was before.*

Reflections: Write a story about running into your ex when you are your best, most fantastic post-breakup self. Are you CEO of a multimillion-dollar company? Married to the finest NFL player in the league? Curing cancer and saving rainforests and looking good doing it? Describe what your success looks and feels like for you. (Think big and be creative!)

Prayer for Release of Anger

Dear God,

I don't apologize for my anger. It's part of the kaleidoscope of human emotions, it's my right to feel it, and I have. I've been mad at my ex, mad at the situation, mad at myself, even mad at you. I've had time to be pissed off, seethe, and plot revenge. But don't allow my anger to consume me. When it no longer serves me to feel this particular feeling, please lift me out of it, God. Don't allow me to hamper my forward movement by basting in it longer than I should or rehash my triggers from the past. Underneath the anger, there's a layer of hurt and, left unchecked, they together can eat away at my health, my spirit, and my mind. I declare a fresh wind of resolution and peace over myself to strip away the intensity of anger and heal the wounds that exist on its underside.

In your name,

Amen

SEVEN

DEPRESSION

Circle of Love

It is one of the blessings of old friends that
you can afford to be stupid with them.
—Ralph Waldo Emerson

On a particularly wretched day, I was on the phone with Keisha feeling feeble and small and hopeless. I was so weighted by despair and gloom, I couldn't even really talk. My vocal cords failed like dry-rotted rubber bands every time I tried to whisper a sad word. About an hour later, she knocked on my door with a half-gallon of cookies 'n' cream, a container of brownie bites, and her listening ears. *That's* a friend.

> **We need people around us** who
> can connect with our spirits and
> love us through the painful places.

I've been abundantly blessed with a super-caring, super-loving, super-close family and a wealth of beautiful friends who are like family. They've each helped me stave off the overwhelm of life in their own unique ways and given me permission to wail and vent, pontificate, repeat myself and apologize for repeating myself, then repeat myself again. Big Sean, Jay, and Kanye have their clique and I have mine. Mine aren't rich (yet) and they don't rap (and shouldn't), but ain't nobody fresher than *my* clique, clique, clique.

Social, cultural, and spiritual conventions say you're supposed to be strong because you're a woman, especially if you're a Black woman, and even more if you're a Black woman of faith. As believers, we're taught to turn everything over to God's loving care and worry about nothing. Except life can get messy and we're wired with responsive emotions that don't always dissipate with the flip of a Bible page. We need people around us who can connect with our spirits and love us through the painful places.

It's tempting to isolate yourself from your friends and family when you're going through heartache rather than burdening them with your melancholy and being the Eeyore of your circle. But social isolation worsens depression and increases reliance on unhealthy coping mechanisms like alcohol and overeating. A study by a professor at University College London even suggests that isolation exacerbates factors that lead to early death. And you, my dear, do not want to die.

Let your homefolk help you, love on you, encourage you. Tell them what you need and express the areas where they can support you. You may struggle with some loneliness, for example, so say something like, "I'm going to need people to hang out with more often because he and I spent a lot of time together and that empty space is going to be difficult for me." Don't let pride keep you sad and lonely.

Women are, by nature, caretakers and nurturers. Allow the same care and nurture you've extended to the folks you love to be reciprocated onto you and allow yourself to receive it.—*J.H.D.*

Affirmation: *I didn't lose love. I gained even more of it from people who prioritize me in their hearts.*

Reflections: Have you been pulling away from family and friends: ignoring phone calls, breaking plans, staying to yourself? It's fine to create space when you need alone time, but how will you know when you've gone too far? Set an intentional goal to avoid slipping into deep isolation— for example, "I will talk to a friend for 30 minutes every day this week" or "I will hang out with my parents on Saturday afternoon."

Wallow in Your Blues—For Now

For everything there is a season, and a time for every matter under heaven ... a time to weep, and a time to laugh; a time to mourn, and a time to dance.—Ecclesiastes 3:1, 4 (NRSV)

Some motivational speakers and preachers can leave you feeling like positive thinking is the only reality of the human experience. I've always been an optimist with a glass-half-full mentality, but there are moments in life when pain-filled, negative experiences make your rose-colored glasses ash-tinted. You know the world expects smiles but when you're heartbroken, you only have tears to offer.

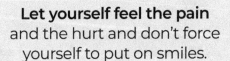

Let yourself feel the pain and the hurt and don't force yourself to put on smiles.

Kelly Rowland uses a word in "Dirty Laundry" that captures the gap between your pain and the happiness of other people around you: *bittersweet*. In the song, she describes how Beyoncé was building an amazing career while, at the same time, Kelly was experiencing the pain of her failing relationship. Her lyrics capture how you can be going through your moment of agony while people you care about are in their greatest revels.

While I was trying to get over him, my goddaughter had her sweet 16, my friend got engaged and had her engagement party, and one of my best friends gave birth to her first child. While my world was falling apart, their worlds were coming together. I was truly happy for them, but I couldn't put on the smiles and celebratory mood necessary to cheer them on for a sustained amount of time. I wanted to be alone. I wanted to cry, or more like Ecclesiastes put it, weep.

I felt guilty for not being able to celebrate, but I couldn't make myself do it. Rarely is your circle all in the same season of happiness or mourning together. The world still beats around you during heartbreak, but you want to shut down. I'm usually solid and even-keeled, riding with my friends and family for the good and bad times, but there are moments when you have to be painfully selfish.

Sometimes there's a voice inside you that will try to convince you that you're a bad person or maybe even outside voices that will cajole you to take one for the team. However, I will not be that voice. Instead, I'm the one telling you to give yourself time to wallow in your blues. Let yourself feel the pain and the hurt and don't force yourself to put on smiles when you're not ready to do it.

Be okay with a season of pain. Acknowledge where you are, share why you can't make it if you want to, and when you're feeling better, make it up to them. Your friends may be hurt, upset, and even sad, but trust that relationships mend and people who love you will understand and forgive you for the moments you just couldn't be there because you were doing the work you needed to do to heal yourself.—*T.H.*

Affirmation: *I accept this season knowing it is only temporary.*

Reflections: Healing will require some selfishness to care for yourself. Write down 10 fun self-care activities you can do to help you heal and then make a plan to do them.

No Words for Prayer

Likewise the Spirit also helps in our weaknesses. For we do not know what we should pray for as we ought, but the Spirit Himself makes intercession for us with groanings which cannot be uttered.
—Romans 8:26 (NKJV)

My heart was so burdened that I could barely eke out one- or two-word prayers fresh into the breakup. This minister (me) who regularly and confidently prays in front of others could barely string together a cohesive set of words to God.

> The **Holy Spirit is giving voice** to prayers you have yet to form.

What do you even ask for when your world is crushed? Do you ask for God to restore your world? Do you ask for a miracle that whisks away the pain of heartbreak? Do you ask for God to get on your side and send a bolt of lightning to strike down your ex? Do you pray that he gets his heart crushed, Marsha Ambrosius "Hope She Cheats on You" style? Perhaps a more eternal prayer request that he be sent to Dante's Ninth Circle of Hell?

It's in these low moments our faith may waver and we feel far from God because we can't find the words to say or even worse, the answers to our requests can't be heard.

In those moments of overwhelm, I'm reminded of the lyrics in Tamela Mann's "Take Me to the King." In it, she acknowledges our weakness during pain and our souls' resistance to just giving up.

Sorrow makes you tired. It makes you question whether you have any fight left in you. Although your faith may feel as if it has no anchor, it does. The song reminds us that what we truly need in desperate times of heartbreak is The Healer.

The Holy Spirit is giving voice to prayers you have yet to form. Praying your strength. Praying your peace. Praying you back from the edge. Praying that your faith will not fail. Praying that you will stand despite the pain. Praying that you will heal and laugh again.

Your emotions may make you feel weak, like you don't have the strength to fight, but that's only an illusion. It's in the moments you feel the weakest that your faith is made the strongest because God's Spirit is activated to lead the way. In our weakest moments, when we can't figure it out, we have the opportunity to lean into God's strength. Even though you may feel disoriented, the Spirit is working to guide, heal, and help you find a greater revelation of I Am.—*T.H.*

Affirmation: *My faith is made stronger in this moment.*

Reflections: Use the story in Matthew 14:22–23 to think about yourself as Peter and your heartbreak as your water-walking moment. What would you call out to Jesus as you felt yourself sinking?

Living with the Memories

Loneliness and the feeling of being unwanted is the most terrible poverty.—Mother Teresa

Boyz II Men's "4 Seasons of Loneliness" captures the trail of memories that link me to my ex. I can track parts of my life by referencing our relationship timeline. The things we did, the places we ate, the people we had double dates with, the conversations we had. In my post-breakup life, I never know what will trigger a memory that leads to a flurry of emotions.

> Unfortunately, memories **don't leave quietly.**

Months after we broke up, I found a piece of his dog's hair embedded in my clothing. Another day, as I was sitting in traffic, the profile of the guy in a car next to me caused my mind to wonder where my ex was at that moment. Finding yourself longing for your ex is common.

Memory triggers will cause you to recall the good times. Those clips of memories lead to smiles, then weeping, then anger. I wish away the old memories that elicit pain and even happiness because I know those moments are gone. Unfortunately, memories don't leave quietly. Instead, they clang around, reminding you of the hollow emptiness you feel

DEPRESSION

because of what used to be. It is in those moments that memories and loneliness collide, forming the tune of a sad love song.

You become acutely aware that where there was a party of two, there is now only a party of one. You sit among friends and their significant others and, even with the best smile and laughter, your mind plays a memory of when you all sat together. Mother Teresa's quote above is a reminder of love's power and how losing it can affect our quality of life.

Remember Psalm 27:10: "My father and mother walked out and left me, God took me in" (MSG). The text offers a ray of hope that God is always with you and places people in your life to fill the void of loneliness: the friend who sends you encouraging messages at the right time, the auntie who prays for your heart to heal, the kids in your life who hug and kiss you. You may be lonely in a moment and miss that person, but you're surrounded by people who care.

Joy comes in the morning when you allow yourself to remember that you're loved and you're not alone. Embrace that truth whenever loneliness tries to creep in and drag you into the slump and pain of heartbreak.—*T.H.*

Affirmation: *I am surrounded by love and embrace the love around me.*

Reflections: What memory triggers cause you to miss your ex? Who is the person you can turn to in your lonely moments?

All By Myself

*Remember: the time you feel lonely is the
time you most need to be by yourself. Life's
cruelest irony.*—Douglas Coupland

"Wake Up Alone" is one of the honest, from-the-gut songs I love Amy Winehouse for giving to the world. It's those first lines, those very first lines, that are so striking because right away, they let me know I'm not the only person who's ever wrestled with the mania of loneliness. I can't quote them directly because permissions to use lyrics are tedious and weird, but basically she sings that she's okay in the day because work and errands and the demands of daily life keep her too busy to wonder where he is.

But nighttime is hard. It's cushioned with quiet and welcomes the thoughts that are deflected by the busyness of the afternoon. In the evening, he is noticeably missing and my mind, no longer preoccupied with deadlines or FedEx delivery times or my daughter's dance schedule, gets stuck in overthinking overdrive:

> *I wonder if he's happy?*
> *Yeah, he's probably happy.*
> *When am I going to be happy?*
> *I wish we were happy together.*

I haven't cried in days. I haven't cried, but I feel dull and colorless inside. There's nothing to feel fluttery or

DEPRESSION

wistful about, nothing to look forward to, nothing to hang my heart on.

I don't want anybody there just to fill his space. Someone must have sounded a silent dog whistle because every used-to-be, never-was, or could-have-been is emerging from obscurity. Guys I talked to in the past, dudes who fell off into that unknown place dudes go when they fall off, old news fellas I haven't talked to in ages are suddenly texting, DM-ing, and generally on high alert.

I admit I have a tragically high rate of dating recidivism. But company for the sake of company isn't really company at all, just another person sharing the same air, and I'm bored with them already. It's hard to use any one of them as a distraction because not a one of them is as good as the ex.

Don't be intimidated by your thoughts, a quiet phone, and an empty bed.

When you're rehashing the what-went-wrongs that led to the breakup, it can be tempting to romanticize the relationship and rewrite the story of y'all. He was amazing. You were amazing together. Good memories become his entire resume and the challenges of the relationship get demoted to inconsequential details. You feel like you'll never find anyone you click with so magically, love so deeply, understand so intimately. You two had cosmic synergy that went above and beyond normal love connections. You are part of each other's souls.

That may be true. It's very possible. It's also possible for grief and loneliness to recolor a relationship that in actuality wasn't as close to perfect as you remember. At one point, Keisha had to check me. She reminded me how I had been the one doing most of the driving to see my ex in our long-distance relationship. How I did most of the compromising, which wasn't really compromise at all so much as giving in to keep the peace. How I had spent many teary conversations and weepy prayers trying to figure out how to make us work.

When you're ready to honestly reflect on the history of your fallen romance, ask a friend or family member who can give you an objective perspective on how it really was. In the meantime, at night, don't be intimidated by your thoughts, a quiet phone, and an empty bed. You are in process.—*J.H.D.*

Affirmation: *Loneliness is uncomfortable, but I won't make decisions for myself from a place of neediness.*

Reflections: Ask yourself: *What is the hardest part about this quiet time?* Be aware of where your mind wanders in this space. Keep track of how many times you think about him and set aside $1 for each instance. Use that money to treat yourself to lunch or a pedicure or a new tube of lipstick.

Prayer for Restoration

Dear God,

Sometimes you hold back the storms and sometimes you allow them to hit full force. This time you allowed the latter. This has been one of the hardest seasons of my life. God, you promised in your word that you work everything together for the good of those who love you, so work all the tears and pain for something greater. God, I know I'm not too broken or have been through too much for you to bring me back, so I'm asking for your blessings to emerge from this heartache and pain with a greater love for myself, greater expectation of love in my life, and new and greater perspectives.

In Jesus' name,

Amen

EIGHT
REFLECTION

Reclaiming Yourself

*I love my past. I love my present. I'm not
ashamed of what I've had, and I'm not
sad because I have it no longer.*—Colette

A breakup forces upon you an unsolicited period of reflection, not just about what went wrong at the end but the wounds that occurred along the way. They are residual hurts from incidents and situations that were intentionally made less urgent at the time for the sake of keeping the peace or that were passively forgiven in the effort to just get back to the loving. You pack them away and carry them with you to the end, but they tend to spill back out as you're counting your losses.

After my first major heartbreak with my college boyfriend, who is also the father of my child, I realized I'd spent at least half of our relationship trying to hold on to him, desperate to make myself lovable so we could be a family. When I finally moved on from that, I nestled into an eight-year-long stretch of comfortable love from a good-hearted man who, paralyzed by his own reservations about marriage and responsibility, just would not propose.

> In all of my relationships, there has been **very little celebration of me.**

109

Then I met a guy I'd gone to college with but never personally knew and found out he was kind and thoughtful and fun, and love showed up unexpectedly again. But his wants and needs took up so much room in the relationship that I shrank inside of it, allowing myself—sometimes sacrificing myself—to get smaller and smaller so he could be and stay happy.

Before the implosion of my last relationship, I hadn't noticed how insecure I'd become because I was in constant competition with other women: the ones I saw him checking out, the ones I anticipated he would check out, the ones I imagined he would check out if he were around and so, in his absence, I would voluntarily check out for him.

In all of my relationships, there has been very little celebration of me—not from the men I loved, not from me. It's a tragic pattern, and it took this last go-around of hurt to notice how it shows up in different ways but ultimately snatches at my value.

Make this the start of a journey to rediscover yourself, who you were before you acquiesced a little, altered yourself a little, bowed a little, shrank down a little, maybe in tiny bits at a time to make things go smoother, to make him feel better, to avoid arguments, to look good on social media, to be mindful of someone else's comments, to fit the mold or the expectations of people around you.

There's a lyric I picked up on in Erykah Badu's "20 Feet Tall" that basically says if I come up for air, I might remember that I'm a giant myself. She's right. It's easy to get so caught up in wanting to be prized by your man that you undercut your own worth in a relationship. Now that it's over, don't minimize how big you are because the math between you two didn't work. That doesn't define you. Who you are—the real you, the you who is you when you're alone as much as when you're involved with someone, the you who magnetizes people and draws out their affections, the you who is your own best company and your most magnificent asset—is a force. Cherish *you.—J.H.D.*

Affirmation: *I deserve to love myself even harder and more passionately than I loved someone else.*

Reflections: Did you ever get lost in a relationship? Were your wants, your needs, your preferences, your hopes—inadvertently or intentionally—made less of a priority than your partner's? Recall an example or two (or three or four) and how each made you feel about yourself. How will you avoid letting that happen again?

Letting Go

Love and kindness are never wasted.
They always make a difference. They bless
the one who receives them and they bless
you, the giver.—Barbara De Angelis

Letting go is a twofold process. You have to release the man and the relationship, then incrementally free yourself of the ideas, notions, and dreams you'd built around both of them. It's double the mourning to no longer be able to touch him and see him and, at the same time, realize the things you expected to happen won't ever play out in real life.

I loved him hard. I said it often and showed it just as much. When he didn't have what he needed, he had it if I had it because I willingly gave it to him. On days when his confidence faltered and his frustration got the better of him, I reminded him how powerful he was. I covered him in prayer (and, to be fair, I know he prayed for me right back) and pleaded with God to direct him toward his greater purpose. When I thought about me and mine, I was just as mindful about him and his.

> When women fall in love, **we generally fall all the way in,** Black women especially.

When women fall in love, we generally fall all the way in, Black women especially. We're fiercely protective of our husbands, partners, and boyfriends because, outside of the interpersonal mechanics of our relationships, there's a system historically committed to imprisoning them, dehumanizing them, traumatizing them, and ultimately destroying them. We work hard to make home—in all of its iterations—a safe, loving space for everyone there.

Because of those issues, Black women's love often comes with an overflow of empathy and, unfortunately, we've also inherited an enormous capacity for letting things slide. That's meant tolerating men's varied expressions of emotion, trauma, and inadequacy, and loving them in spite of what the normal hardships of life and the extra hardships of Blackness turned them into. Basically, we take too much mess.

I was all caught up in a weepy hoot and holler about my sadness when the Holy Spirit said, "You always say you want to be a blessing to someone. So … you were a blessing." It was one of those moments when God serves you so crisply, you can't do anything but shut up and think. It took me a while to be okay with that nugget of revelation. I'd wondered why I couldn't stop being nice to my ex. Now I know it's less about him than it is about me and the kind of loving person I am, in spite of who he was and how he behaved.

I pray for the help to say goodbye a little bit every day. I wrestle with a lot of unanswered questions and unresolved feelings, but I'm thankful that I put love into practice. "Flawed Beautiful Creatures" by Stacy

Barthe reminds me of all the big-hearted women who give the greatest parts of themselves over to love. It's a beautiful thing to sow into people but when it's over, willingly let it go. Don't stay in a space that's emotionally, mentally, or physically unhealthy or unsafe—not for him, not for your family, not for your own heart, not for the sake of children or in the preservation of love. The relationship ended because it wasn't a forever situation for you.

God is the master architect of replenishment. Ask him to refill and restore your ability to love yourself so that you can give out more in a better and more secure circumstance. As a result of your selflessness, God will give you an abundance of love in return.—*J.H.D.*

Affirmation: *It's a blessing to get and give love.*

Reflections: How did your love support and strengthen your ex? Do you feel you got back what you gave? How was it different? Now that the relationship didn't work out, how can you focus on loving the other important people in your life?

Afraid to Love Again

There is no intensity of love or feeling that does not involve the risk of crippling hurt. It is a duty to take this risk, to love and feel without defense or reserve.—William S. Burroughs

When I was a kid and my interactions with boys were far less complex, *nothing* could strike fear into my little baby child heart like "Thriller." Seeing the video for the first time had me and my bed-wetting self sleeping with my mama for what was probably the longest and soggiest week of her life. That was scary stuff. But it was imaginary, made up in the masterful minds of Michael Jackson and director John Landis, and even though it frightened me to my core back then, it was just a passing encounter with fear.

> I don't think I could withstand
> **another broken heart.**

This real-life relationship stuff, though? It's recurring terror: the absence of prospects, the crazy of the dating process, the repetition of opening yourself up again and again, the measuring of how much not-perfect you're willing to entertain. And every time it inflicts chaos, every time the love story doesn't end the way I thought it would, the fear is renewed. After each failure, it gets a little harder and takes a little longer to recover. This one in particular has left me changed and affected. I'm scared in ways that haven't necessarily scared me before.

I'm scared of making another relationship mistake because, truth be told, I don't think I could withstand another broken heart. I don't know what the final fallout would look like, but I think it would shut me down indefinitely.

I'm scared I can't trust my feelings because feelings are what got me into this mess in the first place.

I'm scared I've wasted so much time with not-the-ones that my friends are all going to marry off, one by one, and I'll be the last single girl standing.

I'm scared I can't have everything I want. Does God really give us all the desires of our hearts? At the very same flummoxed time, I'm scared to allow myself to believe that God doesn't. Because once you lose faith in one area, it's easier to lose faith in another, then another, and another. Nothing will be off limits or protected from the domino effect of loss.

Our fears are emotional armor. They shield our vulnerabilities, which makes them somewhat functional, but they also keep us limited. In check. Bound. They block us from hoping for something we're not sure we'll ever have and keep us from wanting to venture out into the new unknown. Fear is normal, but don't allow it to be dominant. Be intentional about moving past it, even in the smallest ways, rather than giving fear the freedom to take permanence in your spirit.—*J.H.D.*

Affirmation: *I am patient with myself while I confront the source of my fears. I pay attention to them so I can keep them from growing.*

Reflections: Make a list of each of your fears about love:

What are you afraid of?
Where did you learn to be afraid of that?
Has it gotten more intense over time?
What has fed it? Is it holding you back?

Love You Better

*The first step toward getting somewhere
is to decide that you are not going to stay
where you are.*—attributed to J.P. Morgan

I've been desperate for clear answers, wishing for an Old Testament Moses and Noah moment that would allow me to hear God's booming, Nina Simone-like voice from on high with a directive or, at the least, a comforting word. There are times when God feels so far away, like a character I've read about more than an actual source of power I know for myself. This is one of those times, inconveniently during a stretch when I need daily reassurance.

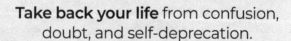

Take back your life from confusion, doubt, and self-deprecation.

To top it all off, I don't have a father or brothers, but I've been craving the insight of a man. I am cocooned in the effervescent wisdom of women, but I knew what my mom, aunties, and friends would all say. Their advice would be tainted by their love for me and empathy for the heartbreak they probably saw coming. They would insist on reminding me how awesome I am and tell me how much better I deserve.

I wanted answers that I wasn't sure were going to be sweet and soft, so I booked a meeting with my pastor, who is prophetic and cool and not so sold out on holiness that he can't be a real-life, regular person too. I trust and value what he has to say and—I can't lie—I was also hoping he could speak on behalf of God in his almighty absence and tell me exactly what I was doing wrong and what would relieve my aching heart. If Jesus wasn't going to fix it, I wanted Pastor to do it.

Seated across from each other in his office, Pastor asked me a series of questions about my life that forced me to unpack my past with uncut candor: how I was teased mercilessly for being overweight and homely when I was a kid, how my first real relationship had also been a physically abusive and emotionally crippling one, how I haven't hit major life milestones fast enough for my liking and always feel years behind where I'm supposed to be at my age.

His magic answer wasn't at all what I expected. He said many valuable things, but this was the gem: He told me I was unhealed and as a result, I was attracting damaged people to me. As soon as he said it, I started to open my mouth and protest, but I ran through my relationship resume right quick. Damaged. Damaged. Damaged. Damaged. My exes didn't exhibit their damage in the same way, but they all were damaged in their own way.

It wasn't the first time I'd heard the concept that hurt people are a lightning rod for other hurt people, but Pastor dropped it on me at the exact time I needed to hear it, which made it a new revelation. I want love back the way I give it out—big, unwavering, and pure—but I need to fix the way I love myself first. I'd been trying to understand men better and God was like, "Nah girl. You need to understand *yourself* better."

This breakup is a moment of clarity for you, your own personal, power-turning "Fight Song" like Rachel Platten sings. Take back your life from confusion, doubt, and self-deprecation. In the midst of the pain, listen to what God is saying. His direction may come in a thunderbolt of insight or it may come in the quiet isolation of prayer. Remain open to hearing it, ask for a credible source of confirmation if you need it, and God will deliver it to you however it's best for you to get it, absorb it, and hold on to it.—*J.H.D.*

Affirmation: *I'm more in tune with myself because of this highly emotional time, and that's a good thing.*

Reflections: Be specific about the kinds of healing you're asking God for. Have you had trouble eating or sleeping? Do you want to release hurts from your childhood? Is there emotional or physical trauma that keeps resurfacing? Meditate on what you need to work on to make yourself full, free, and whole, and be specific in your prayers to ask God to help you concentrate on healing those areas.

Dodged a Bullet

You can't buy love, but you can pay heavily for it.—Henny Youngman

Hollywood ruins some of us. Maybe it's an unfortunate scapegoat, but its greatest export has been the fairy tale that in spite of complications and adversities, naysayers and villains, lopsided timing and inconvenient obstacles, love always wins.

I know better because I live mostly in reality and I've seen how easily a misalignment between two people and a sequence of events can mess up a storyline. But a little, teensy, infinitesimal part of me has clutched onto the hope that my used-to-be will have an epiphany that forces him into uncharacteristic behavior, some outburst of romance that will have him waiting for me on my doorstep when I pull up to my apartment (pouring rain, soaring music, and bouquet of flowers optional). He never is.

This is not *The Notebook* or *Love Jones* or *Brown Sugar* or *Jerry Maguire*. This is unscripted real life, where the plot runs on indefinitely with no rewrites, stunt doubles, or guaranteed retakes. Here, happy endings are the creation of a person who embraces their ability to control their future and their worthiness to live out their vision for their best life.

I admit that I get easily hooked on the magic of what *could be* instead of operating on what *actually is*. I see potential for the man, potential for his qualities, potential for the relationship, potential for a future together, but potential is the most dangerous thing to invest your heart in. It attaches itself to hope and entices your mind to forward-think on things that aren't actually there yet and may never be there at all. Potential itself doesn't do anything. It has all the chill, giving your daydreams something to feed off of without demanding any kind of action to propel possibility into actuality.

Potential can go two ways. It's also possible for a guy to be a pod, an almost-perfect distraction who may initially seem to have everything you need but isn't ultimately who God has set apart for you. I find comfort in remembering all of the times when I was scared of losing something with potential, believing it was the best I could do, before God dropped down and replaced it with another, even better, perfect-for-real thing. It's happened with jobs, laptops, clients, apartments, cars, bosses and, historically, relationships.

> **Potential is the most dangerous** thing to invest your heart in.

So in "Best Thing I Never Had," when Beyoncé sings that she's grateful to have dodged a bullet, I couldn't agree more. I hit the praise button for each and every prayer God has answered with *no*. I thank him for waving me off with a holy "girl, bye" and propelling me through his master plan in spite of me. His interventions are rarely glamorous like an old classic movie or heartwarming like a romantic comedy. But what condition would our hearts be in if God just said *yes*, even if it wasn't the thing he intended for us? I'll take my chances on passing up potential for what's real.—*J.H.D.*

>❚❚

Affirmation: *I don't know why this is happening and why it's happening in this way, but I trust that if I've invited God to head my life, he's got control of this too.*

Reflections: Sometimes situations seem so simplistically and effortlessly logical, i.e., if this would just work out like this, then everything would be okay. When God seems to be saying *no* to your reasoning and your prayers and your asks, what does that do to your faith?

The Good Ol' Days

If I had a single flower for every time I thought of you, I could walk forever in my garden.—Claudia Grandi

You developed a crush on him because he made you laugh in line at the grocery store or he secretly impressed you by answering a question correctly in class. Maybe he made those draggy, impossibly boring days at work seem less draggy and boring, or he helped you when you needed someone to not only care but to show that they did. Next thing you knew, you were in love and however long it lasted, however it came to an end, it had its highs.

> **It's okay to reflect on good times** and appreciate the moments that ushered you **into love.**

During the course of a breakup, we're inclined to make mental voodoo dolls of the dude who's the singular source of our inner turmoil and heartache. Focusing on his bad qualities offers up relief and vindication—screw him and his 300-credit-score, loud-snoring self!—but it's also okay to reflect on good times and appreciate the moments that ushered you into love.

When we give ourselves permission to flash back to the mushy, gushy reasons why we fell in the first place, we not only keep ourselves honest and prevent our pain from recoloring reality, we allow ourselves to remember the wholeness of our experience. In "Memory Lane," Minnie Riperton goes through pictures of her and her old lover, trying to keep herself from slipping back into those old familiar feelings. At the same time, she says she feels the happiness *and* the pain, celebrating both the beauty and the ugliness of the relationship that no longer is.

We may not have made the optimal decision in who we chose to love, but we can take comfort in our ability to see good in others. Very few stories are completely dreamy or disastrous. He may be the villain in your movie right now, but the experience of loving him had value that's worth remembering fondly. That's reassurance that, despite our current despair, we have the capacity to be openhearted. There's opportunity to build on that, add wisdom, and do even better next time.—*J.H.D.*

Affirmation: *I see positives even in hurtful situations.*

Reflection: Think about one of the favorite memories you two made when you were together. What was special about it? Is it difficult to reflect on the good times in your relationship? Why or why not?

Searching for a Real Love

I was seeking a real love, a real deal, and I have been seeking it for a lot of years. And in that seeking, I found that God's love is real.—Dyan Cannon

You may find yourself wondering: *Was it really love on their part?* You will probably recall every conversation, every sweet moment, every phone call, everything you did and everything they didn't do in hopes of trying to resolve the greatest question that Ronnie, Bobby, Ricky, Mike, Ralph, and Johnny ever asked: If it isn't love, then how could it possibly be this painful?

> I hope you land **head over heels** in love with God.

Your tears, sleepless nights, aching heart, and other heartbreak symptoms all testify that for you, it had to be love. But it's almost impossible to reconcile how the weeks, months, or even years of "I love you" from them became (insert dumb statement they used to express the opposite of "I love you").

Some people may contend that love is fickle, that your ex couldn't have possibly loved you if they left, but I believe someone can love you with a deep love and still mess up, walk away, or decide they want something different. Many of us crave intimate love that turns into I-love-you-for-a-lifetime (or at least until I'm ready to say goodbye). However, two people rarely love and let go at the same time. It's that lack of mutuality that hurts us to the core but can be what opens the door to greater experiences of love.

After we seek love and find heartbreak, we can become introspective in the healing process. When we put back together the shattered pieces of our heart, we can begin to truly love ourselves and stop lowering our standards simply to have a bae. You may stumble into the unexpected love of a new friend who wipes your tears as you sob through your agony. You may stumble into the love of a passion project you started to take your mind off heartbreak. But most important, I hope you land head over heels in love with God.

Heartbreak helped me to know God was my foundation because I turned to my faith for comfort. I discovered what the ladies in church mean when they say, "Jesus is a heart fixer and a mind regulator." He restored me and darn sure kept me from losing it on my ex. I also learned what being "clothed in my right mind" means because there were moments I thought I would break from the weight of unrequited love and, heck, just being done wrong. Every experience allows you to encounter God in a different way and offers the chance to go deeper into God's nature.—*T.H.*

Affirmation: *I love God. I love me.*

Reflection: What does real, healthy love look like to you? Is the love you described how you love yourself? Is it how you see your love for God?

Single, Heartbroken Mama

That was way harsh, Tai.—Cher Horowitz,
Clueless

I thought I was doing a pretty good job holding myself together in front of my daughter, Skylar. She was transitioning from middle school to high school at the time and, like most parents of a young teen, I was not the center of her attention or interest. We ate dinner together after school, checked in on each other to chat a few times after she bunkered herself in her room, but mostly I had opportunity to allow my mind to wander. When you're going through a breakup, the absence of viable distractions can lead to overthinking, and overthinking can combust into drama—can and did.

> "Mommy, I can't believe
> you're crying **over a man**."

One weekday evening after we got home from work and school, I had a high-intensity phone conversation with my ex. It started amicably enough but it went south quickly, and I started talking faster and louder until I'm kind of sure I was hollering. It's hard to protect your privacy when you share a wall in a two-bedroom apartment, so when I hung up, I was sobbing and Skylar was standing in my doorway. "Mommy,

I can't believe you're crying over a man," she said, all exasperated. "You're better than that."

As a single mother, the breakup of a relationship is packed with unique elements that pile complications onto a situation already fraught with too many other complications. For two years, he'd been a father figure to her, cooking chocolate chip pancakes for her and helping her with math homework on weekends when we'd visit him and his daughter. It was a little insta-family, me a single mom dating him a single dad, both of us with girls who were about the same age, and everyone got along until we didn't. Skylar has always had a frenetic relationship with her real dad, so I've entered dating situations watchful, cautious, analytical of this guy's worthiness even to be introduced to my child, much less to be around her regularly.

> When you break up with me the mom,
> **you break with my child too.**

Having been on both sides of parenthood—the daughter of a single mother and the single mother of a daughter—I'd taught her the power and value of her young womanhood, and here it came back to roundhouse me in a hurting moment. I was ashamed and embarrassed that she'd caught me in raw despair about anything, especially a broken heart, and a little hurt that she'd judged me in her hypercritical, 13-year-old distaste. I felt like, in one stupid phone call, I'd undone what I tried to instill in her about feminism and independence, especially as a young Black woman. At the same time, I thought, *Wait a minute, ma'am. I'm your mom, but I'm a human being too. And I'm going through it.*

Kids, bless their hearts, ultimately don't care that you're navigating a heartbreak. They're going to want their Cinnamon Toast Crunch or their weekly allowance or a ride to dance practice, and they don't care what you've got going on. The sweetest of them might give you a hug and ask what's wrong, but when it's time to kid, they kid hard. And they should. Because this particular kind of emotional trauma is something most parents and guardians want to shield their children from for as long as humanly possible.

The thing about breakups as a single parent is when you break up with me the mom, you break with my child too, interrupting the stability and consistency she had around a now-failed relationship with another man. That has hurt me deeply every time, feeling like I introduced another play-dad into her life only to disappoint and abandon her. It's never her fault, and I've stressed that to her as many times as I could. But if I'm carrying around disappointment, distrust, and uncertainty, I know she is too. That bothers me.

Skylar teases me about how much I played Chrisette Michele's first album the summer it dropped, and "Be OK" is our theme song and sentiment. God uses what happens to us to come into a full understanding of his love and devotion, and I have to believe if he has a plan for my questions and pain, he has one for my daughter's too. We will be okay. As much as there are lessons and learning for me to incorporate into my decisions going forward, I pray God gives her wisdom in love early so that she doesn't operate out of fear and apprehension, but faith, self-assurance, and an ability to hear and respond to God's direction.—*J.H.D.*

Affirmation: *My kids will grow from this, too, and become more empathetic, emotionally intelligent, and savvy in their own relationships.*

Reflection: What will you teach your children about God's love that they can use as wisdom when they begin to navigate dating?

Are You Ready to Be Healed?

> He said, "Do you want to get well?" ...
> Jesus said, "Get up, take your bedroll, start
> walking." The man was healed on the spot.
> He picked up his bedroll and walked off.
> —John 5:6, 8-9 (MSG)

I've longed to get to the point of acceptance and hope since day one of grieving the loss of my relationship. I wanted to instantly be healed and just get over the emotions and pain. I desperately wanted to stop missing him. I didn't want to long to pick up the phone and joke around or vent about my day, expecting him to make me smile and forget my problems.

I wanted to stop crying, stop the sinking feeling in my stomach, and stop hurting every time I thought about him. I just wanted to accept my new normal and move forward, but I couldn't wish or pray myself to that place where I had perfect peace. Instead, it was a process of good days and bad days.

At some point you'll **finish the process of grieving.**

Know that God will ask you at some point, "Are you ready to be healed from this broken heart?" It may seem impossible to bounce back and recover from heartache because all you see is the pain and the reasons why you invested in this book. Even if it's not today, at some point you'll finish the process of grieving and have that *aha* moment when you realize you've been on the sidelines crying long enough and are ready to get back in the game of life.

Take some time today and listen to the words in Mary Mary's song, "Yesterday." Start saying to yourself: *I am going to put away the tissues. I am going to stop crying. I am done with the misery from heartbreak. That was yesterday. Today I am moving forward.*

Although there is power in letting your tears out, at some point God steps in and says, "Enough crying, daughter. Wipe your tears. Get up out of bed." It may seem simple and pointless to visualize where you want to be, but God has promised you healing for your hurt. So visualize yourself walking in it today.—*T.H.*

Affirmation: *I will survive this hurt. I will wipe my tears and choose to be an overcomer.*

Reflection: What do you want to leave in your yesterday? What do you want your post-heartbreak tomorrow to look like?

Prayer for a Healed Heart

God, come sit with me. Let me be in your presence where healing takes place. It's not time that heals, but it's your presence that restores all that's lost and taken from me in heartbreak. I ask for your peace. Not a temporary peace, but true *shalom* that is the wholeness and essence of your peace. Come through, Divine One, and bring your healing that allows me not to dwell in what-ifs and should-haves, but instead looks forward in hope of new adventures and new beginnings.

God, mend and knit back together my heart so that it's not cracked and chipped and flawed to love again. I pray that this broken heart can be made new. New and full of love for myself and new to love again at the right time. I ask that my heart be free to experience and give the fullness of love to someone deserving of all the adoration and ride-for-you I have stored up inside this renewed heart.

I also pray that you transform this heartache into purpose. I ask that my story of encountering your healing power in the midst of my pain will encourage someone else to know that they too can be healed if they reach out to you. Let my light of healing shine so brightly that I attract those who need to be encouraged by the witness of a person made whole. That is my prayer, that is my desire, so hear my cry, God.

In Jesus' name, Amen

NINE
WORKING THROUGH

Project Restoration

Don't fret or worry. Instead of worrying, pray. Let petitions and praises shape your worries into prayers, letting God know your concerns. Before you know it, a sense of God's wholeness, everything coming together for good, will come and settle you down. It's wonderful what happens when Christ displaces worry at the center of your life.—Philippians 4:6-7 (MSG)

Racing thoughts, abnormal heartbeat, headaches, and deep sighs are all physical symptoms of the anxiety you're experiencing as a result of your world being unraveled. That's why "girl, get over it" is horrible advice. You can't just get over it. You have to be patient with yourself and work through it.

There's something about focusing on God with your whole heart, making the choice to put him at the center of your situation that says, "Despite how I feel physically, I'm going to honor God's goodness." That triggers a shift to peace, even if only temporarily. The more you give yourself permission to focus on God, the less you'll experience those nagging reactions.

> **You can't just get over it.**
> You have to be patient with
> yourself and work through it.

That's not just spiritual feel-good medicine either. Neuroscientists have confirmed that focusing on your spiritual practice causes the brain to produce serotonin. Yep, the low level of serotonin that causes anxiety can be replenished with your spiritual experiences. So the closer we get to our Creator, the more we're supplied with what we physiologically need to return our bodies to peace.

Nothing explains it like the Philippians verse above. When we actively choose to turn our greatest worries and concerns over to God, the Holy One has a chance to replace them with God's self so we no longer focus on the problem, but we begin to see the solution: the Almighty One.

There are three versions of "Fill Me Up," but something about the live version by Tasha Cobbs Leonard leads me into my greatest worship experiences. The song reminds me that I have access to God's total self. When I sit in that presence, the anxieties in my life can be patched so I can live fully.

Right now, you may feel broken, but God is able to mend you and make you a vessel for the Healer to come in and fill. As I opened myself up to God, my tears of heartache turned to joy as God responded to me, inviting his presence to come see about me. Let your prayers, your worship, and your openness to God replace your anxiety.—*T.H.*

Affirmation: *I am making room every day for God to fill me up and restore me to wholeness.*

Reflection: God is listening. What do you want?

Creating Healing Mode

Music was my refuge. I could crawl into the space between the notes and curl my back to loneliness.—Maya Angelou

Much like Mama Maya, music offered me an escape in the midst of heartbreak. It was the chance to turn away from sadness and open up to the fullness of my emotions. I could build a world around the lyrics. I could create a more powerful version of me that wasn't overtaken with despair and loneliness.

Natasha Bedingfield's "Unwritten" embodied that desire to rewrite my story with a happier ending. It set the tone that my life didn't have to be defined by a breakup. Instead, I could create the next chapter forged by my prayers and my actions.

> Find a way to **positively release your imagination** while you grieve.

The idea for this *Headphones and Heartbreaks* devotional came from the healing that music provided as we allowed the lyrics to help us express and release our emotions. That retreat inward gave us creative energy and evidence that God can transform the darkness of despair into a positive force.

Everyone has creative energy, but not all of us harness its potential. Even if you swear you don't have a creative bone in your body, find a way to positively release your imagination while you grieve. Doodle with numbers, paint a room in your house, rearrange furniture, or create a vision board. Find something that activates the creative part of your brain. It forces the memory-dredging part to still itself and turns the loneliness into a place of rest.

You can begin to heal the hurt and make peace with your memories rather than letting them hold you hostage. I have written books after breakups, painted pictures, imagined businesses, and found a great sense of joy and accomplishment while getting over a guy. I channeled my emotions, pain, and confusion into dreams and goals.

It's a process to achieve full healing, but channeling your creative energy through it is worth trying. Maybe you'll have a masterpiece to share with the world. (Wouldn't that be the best thing a breakup could offer?) Even if it doesn't become that, letting your creativity loose allows you to stay busy and ease the pain, if only for a few moments. Plus your success might lead to one day saying, "Suck it! Look at me now!" Okay, that wasn't godly, but you know it would feel good to move your tragedy into triumph.—*T.H.*

Affirmation: *My creative energy is at work within, healing my pain and making me stronger.*

Reflection: Do you believe in the power of being creative? Even if you don't believe, try it. Write a story or a poem. Paint a picture. Do something that expresses your current emotion and the emotional place you want to create in your life.

Sex with the Ex

*If somebody wants to walk out of your life,
let them go ... You're gonna always mess
up when you mix seasonal people up with
lifetime expectations.*—Madea, *Madea Goes
to Jail*

In the context of a relationship, sex is the physical spilling over of all the feelings you have for that person, an expression of your intimacy as friends, lovers, companions, and partners melded into a passionate outburst. That's dope.

When the relationship is over, however, and you keep dipping into that sex well, you entangle yourself in situationship. Few of us are authentically comfortable in it. It's the first cousin of "it's complicated" and it magnetizes messiness, which keeps us emotionally and physically cemented in an expired space. That's not dope.

> **Consider the consequences**
> before you reinvite that man to
> enjoy your magic in any capacity.

Like most well-raised church girls, I was alerted to boys' manipulative trickery so I'd recognize it when it inevitably tried to entice me to experiment with sex.

145

We read scriptures that interpreted how fornication displeased God, accompanied by sermons that further reinforced that premarital sex was flat-out wrong. But having broken that rule the summer before my sophomore year of college, I stayed as close to righteous as I could by only aligning sex with love. I matured into womanhood, but I stayed protective of my number so that, even when relationships had well run their course, I kept recycling my last dude because I didn't want to increase my body count.

Keeping the man you love in your space after he officially becomes an ex is dangerous because sex with an ex is the ultimate gaslighting. If you've been emotionally attached to him, you're probably still emotionally attached to him, and sex only exacerbates that connection. He'll close the deal on sex with you if it's available and offered, maybe even run through the script of what he thinks you want to hear if it makes the possibility more certain. But because you're vulnerable, a one-woman orchestra of emotion like Duke Ellington and John Coltrane's "In a Sentimental Mood," you run the risk of keeping yourself arrested in confusion, hurt, and wishful thinking. I know what it's like. Don't do it, Miss Celie. Don't do it.

Your hormones may flare, you may feel lonely, your rebound dating may be serially disappointing, but consider the consequences before you reinvite that man to enjoy your magic in any capacity. It's a power struggle between the sexual chemistry that you already know works and an ever-so-easy slide back down into emotional hell. Meanwhile, you'll be wasting time and energy. When the romantic feelings fade and you can appreciate him platonically, you may be able to genuinely be his friend. But for now, don't look back.—*J.H.D.*

Affirmation: *I'm committed to holding out for the real thing.*

Reflection: Have you returned to the well for friendship or more? What was your decision-making process? How did you feel afterward?

Social Illusions

We live in a world of communication. Everyone gets information about everyone else. There is universal comparison and you don't just compare yourself with the people next door, you compare yourself to people all over the world and with what is being presented as the decent, proper, and dignified life. It's the crime of humiliation.
—Zygmunt Bauman

The connectivity of social media is a gift and a curse. It's entertaining, it's informative, it's fun to see what your best friend from kindergarten and that dude you crushed on hard in middle school are doing with themselves long after they've become memories. It's certainly made staying in touch easier because honestly, if someone can't tweet, tag, message, DM, post, or comment, it's pretty safe to assume they're roundly unbothered and disinterested in seeing about you.

Stalking his page will only **stoke the pain** you're trying to overcome.

Good as it is for news, catching up, and the occasional debate, social media can easily become the measuring stick you use to size up your own accomplishments and milestones against the perceived accomplishments and milestones of others. It makes folks' lives look as if they're going so much smoother, better, faster, greater, further than yours. One friend gets engaged, another just got married. This one is having a baby, that one is celebrating a 10-year anniversary with the love of her life. Meanwhile, you're bunkered by boxes of Kleenex because you've just broken up with your man and all of those blessings look so impossibly far away and unattainable right now.

Facebook, Instagram, TikTok—all of that is "Fool's Gold" like the song Jill Scott sings. The surface is sparkly and shiny, but the material underneath isn't nearly as pretty and precious. That's not to say there aren't genuinely happy people living amazing, authentic lives. Indeed there are, and good for them. Still, we don't see the sludge they've had to crawl through, perhaps even before social media was a thing, and we don't often hear about troubles brewing behind the scenes at present. Social media is a place to present everything as beautiful. It's an escape from the dues being paid to get or stay happy.

The tricks of the enemy are plentiful. 1 Peter 5:8 (MSG) says, "Stay alert. The Devil is poised to pounce, and would like nothing better than to catch you napping." If you're vulnerable to its illusionary magic, social media can stunt you with self-comparison and stall you out on inadequacy. Particularly in this time when you need to be affirmed, that can be dangerous. Back away from the newsfeed, ma'am. Especially—*especially*—if you've stayed friends (at least in social media terms) with your now ex-love. Stalking his page will only stoke the pain you're trying to overcome. And that's emotional sabotage.—*J.H.D.*

Affirmation: *I will rebuild the sparkle in my own life instead of being impressed by someone else's.*

Reflection: Write a love note to a friend or relative instead of contacting them on social media. Tell them how they've enriched your life or share something you love about them that you may have never told them. Drop it in the mail, pre-social-media style. (Be clear: This does not include The Ex.)

Therapy Isn't a Cuss Word

I love myself. The quietest, simplest, most powerful revolution ever.—Nayyirah Waheed

Prayer is like air and light. The act of putting yourself on pause opens you up to God.

Therapy is like using that air and light to cultivate a garden. It opens you up to yourself.

I started seeing a therapist in standing weekly appointments more than a year before The Crash. I'd been fighting hard to ascend to my next level in life, but I suspected that unresolved baggage I was hauling around from my past was keeping me bolted in place. So I researched therapists, purposefully found a Black woman psychologist, cracked my insides open, and invited her to help me figure me out, one hour, one week at a time.

> The repair process **has to be more aggressive** than the original damage.

There is restoration in prayer. It's quiet time to hear your own heart and get clear on what you're asking God to do. Sometimes in that sacred space of communicating with the Creator, you stumble on answers. Prayer is conversation from the soul and there's no substitute for it.

God has, however, anointed psychologists, counselors, and therapists with the desire and skill to help people sort through varying levels of chaos from their mistreatment, bad relationships, behavior patterns that hinder them, and their own thoughts and experiences. Mental healthcare is as critical as regular exercise and balanced eating because the mind is as much of a source of power as the spirit and the body. We can't be holistically healthy without taking care of it too.

I'm in the process of loving my whole self. My stubbornness. My sometimes overthinking, sometimes impulsiveness. My indomitable acne and its consequential brown spots. My not-round-enough butt. My resilient love handles. My flitty, scatterbrained, housefly-small attention span. My extroverted introversion or my introverted extroversion, depending on the situation and what kind of day it is. All of me. It's not a fast lesson. It's not easy either. When years of not-good-enough intersect with the rejections of a failed relationship (or two or three or four), the repair process has to be more aggressive than the original damage.

My therapist is a patient guide through this transitional phase, and Alicia Keys' "Brand New Me" is a beautifully appropriate soundtrack, especially when she sings that it's taken bravery and time to get to authentic self-acceptance and self-love. That part makes me well up with tears because the struggle has been too real. Eliminating him from my life to make room for lasting blessings makes logical sense, but it's a daily shock of hurt. It has shifted the focus off loving him and reminded me I need to love myself as committedly and passionately. Even more than that.

You are recovering. You may just want to wake up one day and be over it, but the cut has to scab over before it becomes love's war wound. Therapy may help you better process the aftershocks of your heartbreak. Pray through it but ask God to help you seek the professional counsel you need to make the mental recovery that will equip you to become a brand-new you.—*J.H.D.*

≫▯▯

Affirmation: *I am deliberate about becoming completely whole, healthy, and healed.*

Reflection: How do you take care of your mental and emotional needs? What are the benefits of those practices?

Giving Too Much

She stood there until something fell off the shelf inside her.—Zora Neale Hurston, *Their Eyes Were Watching God*

When you need a lesson brought to your attention, Yahweh will throw it in front of you in the most random of ways. Our God is a God of strategic message placement. He'll tuck an *aha* moment into a song lyric, a sentimental commercial, a piece of candy wrapper, the ramblings of a mentally unstable stranger, whatever he has to do to make his point, as many times as he needs to do it in order to get it across.

In no less than three instances lately, he's told me to stop playing wife. Mostly, I suppose, because I'm not one.

Until The Crash, the ex was at my apartment three or four days out of the week. I cooked for him. I revised his resume. I found him a quality medical provider when he signed up for Obamacare— after I helped him sign up for Obamacare—and I researched the consolidation of his student loans. I led the mission to get some minor charges expunged from his record. I filed his fingernails. I exfoliated his elbows.

I said I exfoliated that Negro's elbows, y'all.

In this space of recovery and healing, God is showing me how I've given dudes too much of myself over the past years with little to zero reward besides being drunk in love. I did all kinds of intimate, personal, helpful stuff because helping and caretaking are among my love languages. If I look back from my first real boyfriend to my last one, I've gotten plenty of wife practice but never actually been a wife. The good Lord is telling me to rein all of that in until the one worthy of receiving it steps up with a ring and an authentic promise of forever. Until then, I refuse to cook as much as a serving of Top Ramen for a man who has not proposed.

> **I've given dudes too much of myself** over the past years with little to zero reward.

(The Whispers' "I'm Gonna Make You My Wife" just dropped into my mental jukebox. Future Hubs may not be able to sing—that's not on my list of requirements—but he'll share that beautiful sentiment.)

We expend so much energy mourning the loss of him, let's review for a moment what he lost. He lost you as a champion. He lost your intelligence and brilliance. He lost your quick and creative problem-solving (because we know for sure Black women think fast on our feet). He lost you saving him from himself. He lost your humor. He lost your gestures of love and care. He lost your unique combination of gifts, skills, and talents. He lost your beauty and glow. He lost access to you. And, even if you still pray for him, he lost your active intercession, which invoked favor for him in countless situations.

Use this heart-healing and recovery time to reinvest in celebrating yourself. You've demonstrated in real time that you can be the Proverbs 31 woman (Proverbs 31:10-31), if that's in fact what you were striving to be, or that you're destined to be a dynamic wife if you weren't already. You don't have to prove yourself to the God who's already preparing to blow your mind when you're ready.—*J.H.D.*

Affirmation: *I give out only what I expect to get back.*

Reflection: How do you express love? How do you want to feel in the context of a relationship? When do you feel most loved?

Time to Forgive

*Those who are free of resentful thoughts
surely find peace.*—Buddha paraphrase

One day while I was driving through the city and thinking about how unfair it was that he had already moved on, my thoughts were interrupted by Tenth Avenue North's song, "Losing." It was as though God piped in and said, "Enough whining about wanting him to suffer. What about forgiveness?"

The song acknowledged the wrong I felt had been done to me, but it forced me to embrace forgiveness, the guiding principle of Christianity. Forgiveness is about setting *yourself* free, not about the wrongs of the other person, and that doesn't quite translate to the heart in the midst of unpalatable pain. But now I was confronted with the challenge to ask God to, "forgive them for they know not what they do," like Jesus.

> **Forgiveness is about setting *yourself* free**, not about the wrongs of the other person.

Forgiveness is not easy nor has it been a principle I've readily embraced. It's a practice that I have to actively engage in by reminding myself of messages like the Buddha paraphrase above. Forgiveness is an invitation to put down your need to be "righted" against someone who "wronged" you and enter into a different frame of mind.

As difficult as it may be, I am more peaceful when I focus less on revenge and more on my healing. The mental space I dedicate to how he wronged me and how I want him to be punished inevitably steals my peace and forces me into mental acrobatics about the breakup. You are the only one who can decide to divert your energy from the negative to the light of forgiveness and invest in your inner peace.—*T.H.*

Affirmation: *I choose to walk in the light of forgiveness.*

Reflection: Do you feel you are losing if you allow yourself to forgive your ex for breaking your heart? Could you really be winning to offer forgiveness? What's the hardest part about forgiveness for you?

Live for Yourself

i found god in myself & i loved her/ i loved her fiercely—Ntozake Shange

As mothers and aunties, cousins and sisters, mentors and advocates, and as women in general, we have a vested interest in introducing girls and young women to their beautiful worth. We want them to soar in their personal definitions of success, feel comfortable and confident in themselves, and be free in their individual greatness. We want them to have the affirmation some of us never got or the level of self-worth we once had and lost.

Live a life for yourself and you won't have wasted any time.

There are very adult women—ladies with degrees and good jobs and house notes and their own children to look after—who need that kind of support too. The trauma of a heartbreak can push unresolved pain to the surface and play Jedi mind tricks on how you look at and feel about yourself. After a bad breakup, disparaging narratives from your past plus the fresh emotional wounds can become a joint motive to start picking yourself apart.

If I looked like this, if I were built like that, I wouldn't be single.

If I had made this amount of money, if I had accomplished that goal, I would've been a better partner.

If I acted more like a lady, if I weren't so independent, if I were softer, if I were harder, if I were louder, if I were quieter, if I were sexier, if I were smarter, I'd be more lovable.

Growth and introspection are healthy, but anything that comes from a place of faultfinding in the pursuit of comparative perfection is not growth or introspection. When the script in your mind starts playing back negativity you've heard or said about yourself, it poisons your spirit and stunts your healing.

Relationship "experts" are making millions of dollars impressing on women what they need to do, be, say, wear, think, and believe in order to qualify as marriage material. It's another layer on the already exhausting weight we carry trying to be just right. If you do something new—learn a skill, develop a quality, enhance a trait—don't do it because you think it'll better prepare you to be a wife. Do it because you want to do it for *yourself*.

I double love J. Cole for writing "Crooked Smile." It's not typical for a male rapper to empathize with the pressures put on women, then turn around and celebrate us as we are. The whole second verse is a tribute to us. You, dear heart, are an amazing work of Black girl brilliance, no matter how old you are. Be especially careful about what you're telling yourself and the flaws you allow your pain to draw your attention to.

The days waiting for The One can get long. Live a life for yourself and you won't have wasted any time. If a loving relationship, even a spouse comes along, bless

God. If not, you will still have lived and not missed out
on the things you could control.—*J.H.D.*

Affirmation: *My goal is wholeness, not perfection.
I'm intentional about building and protecting my
confidence.*

Reflection: Is there any unresolved pain from
your past—old relationships, childhood traumas—
emerging to be handled once and for all? How will
you confront and slay them?

You've Got the Power

Never underestimate the power you have
to take your life in a new direction.
—Germany Kent

I don't know when Jay-Z messed around and got caught. But I know men have been acting up for a long time and creating tears for women. That's why I can still remember the day the *Lemonade* album dropped in 2016, because Beyoncé voiced relationship woes I related to. I was sitting on the sectional in my mom's house. I cried, danced, and texted Janelle. If Queen Bey could experience this, then we didn't have to feel bad, and the reality was that men were big poo-poo head dummies.

> **You have the power** to hold your head up, shift your life into a new direction, and move on.

There's something epic and cathartic about the lyrics. Let's be clear—I'm definitely in the Beyhive. But I'm also convinced she was anointed by the Spirit when she penned and recorded *Lemonade*. It is still, for me, *THE* album. The one I refer to nonstop. The one I listen to when I am hurting and when I need inspiration, when I'm angry and when I feel love. I just remember having it on repeat and the heaviness of trying to claw myself out of heartbreak would get a bit lighter with each listen.

"Sorry" became my anthem, and it's still my go-to angry song. It might be the church girl in me who was raised not to cuss, but I feel empowered whenever I sing it to put my middle finger in the air. I feel rebellious. Resilient. Defiant. It gave me all the energy I needed to be stronger than my ex, who by that time had moved on and was back with his ex-girlfriend. He didn't even know I was imaginarily flipping him off, but it didn't matter to me. I got the power I needed.

I don't know when you'll arrive at the *aha* moment that helps you realize you have the power to hold your head up, shift your life into a new direction, and move on. Ecclesiastes 3:1 assures us, "There is a time for everything, and a season for every activity under the heavens." This is your season to divert your attention away from your ex and toward creating the life you want.

Use the empowerment of Queen Bey and other women who have mustered the strength to pick up the pieces after the mess of a heartbreak. You don't have to be sorry for wanting more. Every day, try to replace a thought about your ex with a thought about what's next for you. Take back your power and move the hell on.—*T.H.*

Affirmation: *I am powerful. I have the power within to create a new path for my life.*

Reflection: What makes you feel powerful? Start to incorporate that into your daily routine. Personally, I have a daily affirmation playlist that hypes me up. The songs remind me that I'm a dope woman who is unstoppable. It could be as simple as wearing makeup and admiring yourself in the mirror, then reclaim that and beat your face like it's date night every day.

Facing All the Risks

It sucks when you get your heart broken by someone and you didn't even get a Celine bag out of it.—My friend Charlie

God speaks in my church, and he often chooses me to speak to. Still, not every message is for me so one Sunday, when my pastor reminded the congregation, "You've got to be ready to take a risk," I shrugged it off inside. Pastor is anointed but, I thought, *That Word isn't for me. I like traveling and trying new activities. I've been self-employed for years and Lord in heaven knows that's a daily risk. Chile, I take risks all the time.*

As I was coming up out of my mental pat on the back, the very next thing out of Pastor's mouth was: "Take a chance on love again. Love even harder next time. I know you've been hurt but stop playing it safe."

Now wait a minute. Y'all, God got jokes. Obviously, love was a type of risk I hadn't considered. But it is indeed a risk.

> I have to be willing to accept an **entire menu of risk.**

I do miss being in love. I miss the euphoria of seeing his name pop up on my phone and the rush of excitement in hearing him pull up outside because I know exactly how his car engine sounds. I miss the cuddling and the pillow talk, the playfulness and the intimacy. I miss those long, smoldering hugs, the kind where you inhale each other and just sink into his body. I miss knocking around the house in a shirt I hijacked specifically because it smells like him and knowing him well enough to ask a server not to put pickles on his burger because he hates pickles on his burger. I miss the comfort of sharing a special someone's company.

To get to all of that though, I have to be willing to accept an entire menu of risk. Even being open to being open to it is scary. But I'm starting to become more comfortable with the realization that I don't want to stay locked into fear, resentment, and fury much longer. I think I'm ready to let it go. When I first noticed the thought, I shoved it away because the fear, resentment, and fury have been familiar, justified, even protective. They've been my emotional barbed wire, blocking me from prospective interlopers and even a whiff of their drama. But sustained anger is heavy and now I just want to be light.

In "Self," Cleo Sol asks God to help her be gentle with herself and convert her rage into peace. I feel that. At the beginning of starting over, battles of the mind can be especially overwhelming. Our healing starts when we release the wall of emotions we built up at our most vulnerable points. Honestly, I'm not even sure how to begin dismantling mine. Maybe I start by disarming all of my regrets, mistakes, and shoulda, coulda, wouldas. How free would we all feel if we extended ourselves even a fraction of the grace that we've volunteered to other folks, especially and most particularly our exes?

There's risk in believing new things about yourself, your life, and God. There's risk in forgiving yourself for decisions and behaviors that didn't serve you well. There's even a risk that, all this wisdom and hard-earned learning aside, you might make the same mistakes again. God has power over time and quantity, and whatever measure you have of the virtues you need—patience, courage, self-love, faith—is more than enough if you place it in God's hands. That means old beliefs and concerns and fears associated with dead relationships can fall away if you let them. So let them.

And when you're ready, forgive whoever you need to forgive to reclaim your sparkle, your wholeness, and your peace of mind. Most important, girl: Forgive yourself.—*J.H.D.*

≫❚❚

Affirmation: *I am thankful for taking the risk to feel love, receive love, and experience who I am in love. It took courage to get there.*

Reflection: What are you telling yourself about yourself? Where is that coming from?

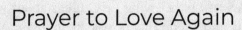

Prayer to Love Again

Dear God,

Clean off the residual tarnish of unbelief that's been left behind by heartbreak. Lift me above the doubt that I'll ever find love again. I'm crying out, asking for the courage to overcome the fear of being vulnerable with you, myself, and people in my innermost circle. Although my walls are up and my heart is on lockdown because of this blow, I don't want to stay in this broken space forever.

Remind me of all the things that made love great. Help me to begin this journey back to love through self-discovery by learning exactly what I want in a mate. Heal my heart so it can be open to the possibility of new love and the joy it brings. Give me the courage to embark on a journey of love when it presents itself. It won't be easy to love again, but I stand on the promise that you can make all things new (2 Corinthians 5:17) and that I can overcome all the hurt and pain. I can look forward to your adding greater into my life as I put you at the center (Philippians 3:13, 4:7).

God, I don't know that I'm ready now, but I'm open to the gift of love entering my life again. Love that will wipe away the tears I've cried by adding happiness to the new memories we'll build together. Amen.

TEN
RECONSTRUCTION

Choose the Road to Recovery

There is no recovery for anyone without lifting the lid on the pain of the past and letting in the light.—Rob Lowe

Obsessive. That's the word I would use to describe my mental state during the early stages of my breakup. I replayed every word. I reevaluated every sign I might have missed. But to heal, I had to accept what happened and move forward one day at a time until I wasn't obsessing anymore, until I wasn't crying anymore, until I could mention his name and reminisce about the good times without emoting.

Danny Gokey, a former *American Idol* finalist, wrote "Tell Your Heart to Beat Again" as a reminder that your life's story will not be this pain. Starting over is always an option you can choose, no matter how great the painful experience.

God is at work, but you have to actively participate in your healing. You choose how this road to recovery goes. The stronger you get each day, the more you can tell yourself to let go and embrace God's hope of a future you can't yet see. The lyrics remind you that you can say goodbye to where you've been and what you've experienced.

God is at work, but **you have to actively participate** in your healing.

You can't heal by passively waiting on God. It requires actively believing, working, and engaging yourself to not be locked into your pain. Use faith, prayer, reflections, and affirmations to let go of one stage of healing and progress to the next. Moving forward won't always be easy. At times, it'll feel like you've slipped backward. In fact, as I'm typing these lines, flutters of emotions are stirring and a few tears emerged, but I've moved so much further along and so have you.

Don't let this painful experience be the end of your story. Let it be the impetus to the next song in the soundtrack of your life or the next chapter you write in your story.—*T.H.*

Affirmation: *I release pain, anger, and hurt from my heart. I am ready to attract joy into my life.*

Reflection: What can you tell your heart to let go of and begin again? Write your future self a letter about where you are now and where you'll be a year from now.

Let Go, Let God,
Let Go Again

If you're brave enough to say goodbye, life will reward you with a new hello.—Paulo Coelho

Sometimes when we invite God to take over a situation, we're only temporarily ready to relinquish control. In a flash of frustration or despair, we beg God to lead and then, once we've recovered from that momentary hiccup in our autonomy, we sneak back into the driver's seat. I've done it at least three dozen times—maybe three dozen more than that— trying to pull myself out and away from broken relationships and their consequential heartaches. And the good Lord obliges me every time until I'm ready to complete the cycle again.

A few years ago, Erykah Badu posted a video on social media giving advice for moving on from a relationship in the hilariously curt, it-is-what-it-is way she has. "You gotta go all the way through it ... If you don't want to let go yet, keep on calling and getting hung up on. Keep on following him around and getting embarrassed," she said. "You gotta get your weave snatched out a couple more times ... When you get tired enough, you'll evolve. I promise."

The inability to let go for good comes from fear— fear of loss, fear of abandonment, fear of loneliness, fear of missing out on something that in actuality may not have been intended for you in the first place. Instead of exacting the desired result, every tactic implemented to hold on to that relationship usually ends up making the situation worse. It's like your bus is pulling away from the curb at a high rate of speed and you're gripping on to the rear bumper for dear life. Girl, that's not what God wants for any one of his daughters.

> The inability to let go for good **comes from fear.**

This much I know: When you're emotionally exhausted from taking running leaps into big brick walls, you'll give it over to God—and leave it there. When you're all cried out and sobered up from your love drunkenness, when you've analyzed and investigated from every reasonable angle and a few more that don't make any good godly sense whatsoever, when you have tired of brawling with your own insides, you'll invite God to intervene and let him do it. Then you'll know you're done. Then you'll know you're really ready to let go.

In 1988, Aaron Hall belted out the lead vocals in "Goodbye Love" with his two bandmates in Guy and it's been a classic ever since. But *goodbye* is also a necessary sentiment. You can say it as many times as your lips will form the word, but the real release comes only when you absolutely mean it.—*J.H.D.*

Affirmation: *When I really give it over to God, I leave it there.*

Reflection: Are you really finished with the relationship? How can you tell? Have you invited God to take charge of the situation? What happened when you did or didn't?

Your Inner Lotus Blossom

God never allows pain without a purpose.
—Jerry Bridges

Beauty can emerge even in the untidiest life moments. I admire the lotus flower not only for its beauty but for the symbolic story behind its growth process. The pure white petals suggest it may originate in a pristine pond. It's quite the opposite. Instead, they emerge from the murkiest of waters. It reminds me that the Creator has an amazing way of using the messiness in our lives to birth the most beautiful things if we're open to trusting the process.

> The Divine can reveal to you the ways **this moment can be made purposeful.**

You may not imagine right now that God can take the agony you're feeling to ignite your superhero status. The Spirit will activate a bloom within you for your personal growth and to be imparted to someone else. God's purpose is always dualistic. It serves us and it causes us to serve others. Though you may have found yourself asking God "Why me?" I invite you to ask God, "What are you teaching me and what do you want me to share with someone else from this experience?"

There are two biblical passages that ask the question: Is anything too hard for God? (See Genesis 18:14 and Jeremiah 32:27.) The answer, of course, is no, nothing—including taking the broken pieces of your heart, putting them back together, and creating within you the power to soar. I'm not promising you another love but something greater. A greater awareness of who you are in God. A deeper understanding of who God is to you. The opportunity to let God spark within you a shift from your greatest moment of desperation to your greatest inspiration.

I believe eventually the Divine can reveal to you the ways this moment can be made purposeful. It may be that you grow in your relationship expectations, it may be that you drop it in a sermon or book, or you may give advice to a young girl who comes behind you.

The packaging for "Superheroes," a song by The Script, reimagines the Man of Steel moniker to help listeners invoke the strength we all have within us. The lyrics introduce us to heroes who developed their powers and hearts of steel by experiencing life's knocks. I know you may not feel it now, but you're learning in this painful situation to be your own superhero and discover your own superpowers. Your greatness is emerging because you can find purpose despite your pain.

I believe in your superhero status. I believe you are getting ready to fly and create magic that is beyond your comprehension. Because if God allowed it into your life, then God will help you use it for good. Just wait on it.—*T.H.*

Affirmation: *I'm a hero, I'm a survivor, and I have purpose that is revealing itself in this heartbreak.*

Reflection: Is it hard to imagine that God makes all things beautiful, even the pain of heartbreak? If God led you to someone with a broken heart today, what could you say to encourage them?

Partnering with God to Heal

*"It was a mistake," you said. But the cruel
thing was, it felt like the mistake was mine,
for trusting you.*—David Levithan,
The Lover's Dictionary

Love your neighbor as yourself is one of the affirmations
we say weekly in my church. It's a reminder that God
calls us to value one another in a way that is true to
how we would value ourselves. It is that same love
that I take into an amorous relationship and expect
in return.

What is love without trust? You trust the person to
take your love and treasure it as an invaluable gift. It's
trust that creates the belief that your partner will love
and treat you just as they want to be loved and treated.

Yet somehow even the most churchgoing, praying-
est of saintly people fool around and break women's
hearts. Yes, we all sin and fall short, but I don't want
my heart to be the thing fallen short on. I want some
guarantees that if I pray and they pray, I can trust that
I will avoid heartbreak. Alas, that's not always how
the story ends.

Betrayal comes in different forms. It's lies, it's
cheating, it's the fact that they really saw you as a
meantime and didn't let you know. In whatever way
the breakup went down, you probably feel some level
of betrayal. In the wake of that devastation emerge the
emotions Drake rap-croons about in "Trust Issues."

> Yes, we all sin and fall short, but I don't want **my heart** to be the thing fallen short on.

But good churchgoers know God heals all—in time. (Insert long, deep sigh about the meaning of *in time*.) Unfortunately, the process leading up to healing is pitted with misadventures: side-eyeing people who try to holla, batting away comments that "there aren't any good men," even discovering that the people you thought were good are guilty of betraying their significant others. Betrayal robs you of innocence, hope, and the amount of trust you place in potentials and relationships.

Humanity's innate resilience leads us to create protective mechanisms, and the heartbroken are no different. Mistrust is an instinctual response to protect oneself from pain experienced during the breakup. I may not want trust issues, but I have some. You may have some too because of life's hurts. But at least you know where you are emotionally. Once you have identified your feelings, take them to the Healer and ask to be mended so you can fully trust and love again.—*T.H.*

Affirmation: *I trust that honest, reciprocated love will come into my life.*

Reflection: Have you noticed yourself saying or thinking things that suggest you're not quite as trusting post-breakup?

The Other Loves in Our Lives

I'm not going to tell you to get over it. I'm going to help you get through it.—Stephie Pahlavi Zan

When you're in a love crisis, it's easy to become so wholly consumed by your crushed feelings and volatile circumstances that you neglect to see about the people you love. You're disappointed or frustrated or angry or hopeless, and even though you're available to your loved ones when they're in dire need, you're not doling out your usual little niceties like checking in to see how that job interview went or calling just to say *Hey*. You're understandably self-absorbed and tussling with your present reality.

The hardest part of this breakup journey for me, aside from that whole battered heart and messy life interruption thing, has been watching my best friend go through her own heartbreak. I pray for her. I maintain a ferocious expectation that her dreams will be unleashed. I speak a healing over her that leaves her even better than she was before and an emergence of blessings she never even thought to pray for. Lee Ann Womack's "I Hope You Dance" always chokes me up a little because the lyrics are such a tributary heart song from one person to someone else. They remind me of Keisha.

In the midst of your emotional rebound, it's helpful to invest in care and concern for others, even if you aren't feeling all that sociable or chatty. A small gesture can do a miraculous thing because the Universe has a way of compelling you to think of someone at the exact time they need it most. Even as you piece your romantic love back together, your agape love is still needed and welcomed in other relationships.

> In the midst of your emotional rebound, **it's helpful to invest** in care and concern for others.

We're all intermittently faced with our own heartbreaks and they're not always related to an unraveled romance. Health diagnoses can be heart-breaking. Financial struggles can be heartbreaking. Acting-a-fool children can be heartbreaking. Take just a few moments to channel your prayer power and positive energy into someone else's situation. God cherishes the prayers of the bewildered and adores the selfless act of speaking intercessory power into the lives of others. And, in sending strength and positive energy to someone else, you'll be simultaneously encouraging yourself.—*J.H.D.*

Affirmation: *I activate the healing God power in myself when I pray for someone else.*

Reflection: Have you prayed for someone else today? Who is on your mind or heart to lift up to God, even for a few moments?

Find Your Closure

I think it's important to have closure in any relationship that ends—from a romantic relationship to a friendship. You should always have a sense of clarity at the end and know why it began and why it ended. You need that in your life to move cleanly into the next phase.—Jennifer Aniston

At some point, we've all had the K. Michelle feeling like, "Maybe I Should Call." True love is a funny thing. It can exist through time, distance, and even heartbreak. Fresh into a breakup, the best advice you can get is don't call, don't text, don't inbox him, don't email him.

But one day, I decided I was in a good place and wanted closure on my terms. I know, I wrote in the section on pain to stop looking for closure. Even all this time later, I agonized because I was afraid to fall back into the funk. I was afraid he would reject my call and what that would mean. I was afraid to hear that I never meant anything and what I thought we had was all in my head. My own agonizing, my mother's and friends' assertions not to call, all had me feeling as if calling was not the answer. But the deep desire to do it wouldn't quit.

It was not answers I needed but **the power to make a decision** for myself.

I prayed and waited to feel peace in my heart about my decision to call. Eventually, I knew it was the right decision for me. I called, we talked, he apologized again, and somehow at that point I could accept it. More important, the call made me realize it was not answers I needed but the power to make a decision for myself. It was taking control of the situation and having my say from a place of power rather than teary desperation. It was my release, and I had the closure I needed.

Maybe you should call, maybe you should write a letter that you never mail, but find your closure. I can't tell you that you should or shouldn't call and neither can anyone else. Look deep within and find your truth. Ask yourself why you are calling. Are you strong enough to enter into a conversation without the expectation of reuniting? Will this cause you more pain than healing? Depending on your answer, your closure may need to be "No, I won't call." But whatever your response, at some point you have to make peace with the relationship and accept that it served its purpose and now has ended.—*T.H.*

Affirmation: *Today, I will take back my power. I will close the chapter on this part of my life the way I want to and not the way anyone else says I should.*

Reflection: Do you think closure is needed? Or do you think ending the relationship is closure enough? What do you feel is the best way for you to find closure? Do you have any fears about the finality that may bring?

Prayer for Forgiveness

Dear God,

Yesterday is done, today is mine to walk in and plant the seeds for my future. I ask you, God, to help me let go of guilt and shame for every compromise I made to make my relationship work. Help me forgive myself for every decision I made that in my gut I knew was wrong. I will not look back with feelings of regret for actions that were contrary to my values and core beliefs for the sake of love. Instead, I choose to see it as an opportunity to grow and be wiser. I'll use this as information for me and someone else in the future.

I even forgive myself for the decisions I made and the actions I took after the breakup because I was hurt and responded accordingly. You gave me fullness of life, so I will not walk in shame and guilt. I forgive me just as you have forgiven me.

Now I pray for the courage and grace to extend forgiveness to my ex. I free him and myself, so I no longer wish payback and vengeance for him. Instead, I pray your grace and mercy and transformation in his life so he can choose differently and not inflict this pain on anyone else. Help him to do better. God, in releasing him and myself, I pray that you'll bring greater love and greater joys into my life so I can celebrate your blessings without anger, bitterness, and resentment.

In Jesus' name, Amen

ELEVEN

ACCEPTANCE AND HOPE

The Promise of Love

Celebrate endings—for they precede new beginnings.—Jonathan Lockwood Huie

With time comes healing and with healing comes hope. Just because one person didn't choose you as their forever doesn't mean that you'll never find love again. The possibilities in your future and what you want your next to be emerge as your heart heals and you realize that with the ending of one love story, the chance for another to write itself begins.

> I hope you believe that **God hasn't closed the door** on your possibility of love.

Chrisette Michele's lyrics in "Love Won't Leave Me Out" express the hope of greater love. The once-brokenhearted can become the mended, and the mended can believe in the promises of God. During our very first heartbreaks, Janelle and I would celebrate whenever we saw a rainbow in the sky. It was a reminder that God was still active in our lives and there was more love to experience. The promise and hope of new love was still out there. The appearance of a rainbow after the darkest storm symbolized that, after all the tears had fallen, brighter days of new love would emerge for us too.

It's hard to imagine that the ending of what once seemed so perfect could open the door to a new, even more perfect beginning. But I believe in upgrades and I hope you do too. I hope you believe that God can still bless you and hasn't closed the door on your possibility of love.

You have the opportunity to experience greater love if you use this time between your old relationship and your next one to self-evaluate. Focus more on what you want in your next relationship and what, in hindsight, you didn't want in the last one. Taking time to think it through will avoid creating an obstacle course for the next guy to go through to get to your heart. This is the opportunity for you to find your best, which is linked to God's best.

When you reflect on your relationship with your ex, what thoughts has God shown you about how you deserve to be treated and loved? Beat back disparaging thoughts that may pop up—regrets that plague you or fears that he was the best you can do.

Love won't leave you out! Begin letting go of the hurt and the pain and watch yourself emerge more determined that you'll love again. Today, make a promise that when love presents itself, you'll allow yourself to fall even more deeply. Promise yourself that you'll let the hope of a new love encircle you and you'll breathe it all in, savoring every moment of your new beginning.—*T.H.*

Affirmation: *Love will find me again and I will let it in.*

Reflection: What have you learned about yourself and relationships from this heartbreak? Have you put walls up and hoops in place for the next person to jump through? What would a better love look like for you?

You Deserve Your Love

If you have the ability to love, love yourself first.—Charles Bukowski

My ex candidly told me that he just couldn't be who I needed him to be, although that would be the best version of himself. Those lines should have affirmed my inner worth and had me pulling out the makeup bag, hot outfit, and sexy pumps to head out and find his replacement. But it didn't. As much as I know my wonderfulness, thoughts of *Why not me?* began to take root.

During our relationship, I'd wrestled with core values that I refused to budge on. Self-doubt clouded my self-assurance, and I wondered if I were different, would that have produced a different outcome? If I had been more pliable, would he have stayed? But if someone is worth my love, they would not try to change me physically, emotionally, mentally, or spiritually. I came to the realization that I was giving the person who said goodbye the power to define who I should be rather than looking within for the marvel that God created and is perfecting.

My ex was unwilling to change, and yet I was the one thinking about changing to keep him. When I stepped out of my hurt, I realized

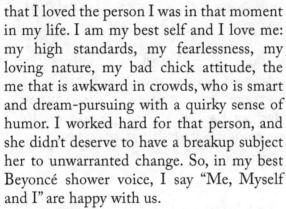

You deserve your love
more than he did.

that I loved the person I was in that moment in my life. I am my best self and I love me: my high standards, my fearlessness, my loving nature, my bad chick attitude, the me that is awkward in crowds, who is smart and dream-pursuing with a quirky sense of humor. I worked hard for that person, and she didn't deserve to have a breakup subject her to unwarranted change. So, in my best Beyoncé shower voice, I say "Me, Myself and I" are happy with us.

I challenge you to remember the same despite how much you may want to think there's something wrong with you. You are not perfect. No one is, but you have to decide whether you love even your imperfections. Chances are, you loved some of his imperfections or, at the very least, looked past them. Don't allow this breakup to define you. You are great. Whatever still needs work, commit to it for the love of you, not your ex or any other relationship.

Embrace the fullness of your worth. You deserve your love more than he did. In the words of Queen Bey, in the end all you have is you. Love you, be your own best friend, and champion yourself.—*T.H.*

Affirmation: *I love me from the inside out, imperfections and all. I rock simply because I AM made me.*

Reflection: Respond to all the negative thoughts, doubts, ideas, and perceived flaws you've been picking apart, even the ones your ex may have pointed out. Have an affirming dialogue with yourself in response to those thoughts.

Adore Me

The course of true love never did run smooth.—William Shakespeare

There's something about "Adore" that makes my heart swell every. single. time. I hear it. My automatic reaction whenever it comes on: Close my eyes, throw my arms up, snap my fingers, and sway like somebody's tipsy auntie at a basement card party. I'm a fan of that little man named Prince anyway, but he hit on every sense with that song. It makes me envision the sight, smell, sound, taste, and sensation of that I-just-can't-help-it kind of love.

Anytime a man says something like, "If God struck me blind, girl, I'd still see your beauty and"—wait a minute, I'm not finished—"I'll be there for you until the end of time because this four-letter L word isn't close to being strong enough to describe what you mean to me," you can believe that dude is out of his mind with adoration. That title is appropriate.

"Adore" was supposed to be the first song we danced to at our wedding reception. It had special meaning for us as a couple. I'd mentioned that I loved it during one of our getting-to-know-you phone conversations and, when we went out on our second date, he played it as soon as I got in his truck. It was such a sweet and thoughtful gesture, and I'm pretty sure that was the day I started slipping into love. (Also worth mentioning: He brought with him a compact of Studio Fix makeup in my shade that I'd told him in passing was sold out at my local MAC store. Bonus *bonus* points.)

> This is the most important:
> **I have to see the God in him.**

Usually songs with an emotional memory attached would be off limits, mentally tossed out because they were part of the soundtrack for a relationship that didn't end in predicted bliss. But I can't throw this particular baby out with the bathwater. "Adore" is still special to me. Some days, when I allow myself to be hopeful, I imagine there exists a man who will feel that way about me, the one who will make me comfortable enough to trust-fall backward into love again.

I'm clear on what I want. He'll make me laugh, even when we're broke, even when we're challenged, even when we're plucking each other's nerves. He'll be intelligent and quick-witted because I'm always here for great conversation and feisty banter. He'll be proud of who he is and grateful for his journey, oozing with integrity and honesty and faithfulness. He'll want to take care of and protect me—physically and emotionally—even though I can take care of and protect myself. He'll be a mature, thoughtful decision-maker. He'll be sexy in his unique way. He'll be charming and supportive and have the kind of manners that will make me personally thank his mama and daddy. His best qualities will balance and complement mine.

There are other things, too, of course, but this is the most important: I have to see the God in him. I need to know that he seeks God for himself, me, our relationship, our children, our household, our extended families. That's what's been missing. The dudes I've dated and loved have been acquainted with God, but they haven't been chasing his favor or his face. If I'm going to commit to sharing my life with someone, I need him to match me in that area. It matters because—it's not just an old church saying—God is indeed the head of my life. And I need any man inserting himself into my and my child's little two-person world to prioritize God too.—*J.H.D.*

Affirmation: *Because God already adores me, he will send me a man who adores both of us.*

Reflection: Prince gives us a single but powerful word—*adore*—to describe how he felt about the one he loved. Pick one word to meditate on for your ideal relationship. Write it on Post-its and keep one in your wallet, put one on your mirror, anywhere you can be reminded about the kind of love you're expecting God to deliver.

Spirit Won't Let You Stay Stuck

Why am I discouraged? Why am I restless?
I trust you, Lord! And I will praise you again
because you help me, and you are my
God.—Psalm 42:11 (CEV)

I'm sure the writers of Psalms never imagined that one day, a heartbroken woman would find herself reading them to find solace. For me, they capture the raw emotion that life produces and the feeling of overwhelming despair that presses you into a place where hope doesn't seem it can be found.

> There's a future **waiting to be experienced** that you haven't imagined yet.

You may have noticed yourself looking at preachers telling you to praise your way out, and snarling back at them or giving them a blank stare because coming to church or turning on the TV to watch a service is all you could muster up. As stuck as you may feel, the Spirit of God within us will not let you stay there. Instead, the Spirit wills us forward to hope even though we can't imagine what our future looks like.

Danny Gokey wrote "Hope in Front of Me" after the loss of his first wife. His testimony is powerful and reminds us of the hope for life after our darkest and most painful moments. Though breakups and deaths are different, they both require knowing that if you wake up to a new day, you still have more life to live, even if the person you love is not going to be by your side.

When you turn your hope to God, you help to initiate your healing. It's a shift from the void and hopelessness caused by heartbreak to the hope that God will heal your pain. It signals to the pain in your heart that there's a future waiting to be experienced that you haven't imagined yet.

Knowing the Creator of life and possibility is beside us in the midst of this storm, willing us into a space of hope for our future, is a powerful visual. Even if your feelings of discouragement, despair, and sadness are trying to snatch your hopefulness, embrace the faith that you aren't at the end. Harness the power of hope and see yourself at the end of the pain. God has the ability to transform your life and reimagine your future.—*T.H.*

>〉❙❙

Affirmation: *My future is brighter than I can imagine because God is already there before me.*

Reflections: What hope would you ask God to give you now?

This, But Better

This is what I know. Don't settle for 40, 50, or even 80 percent. A relationship shouldn't be too small or too tight or even a little scratchy ... It should be perfect for you. It should be lasting. Wait. Wait for 100 percent.—Deb Caletti

Think of the things you adored about your ex. Yes, what you loved.

My ex was hilarious. He made everything fun. We would do a Walmart run or go get gas or pick up a pizza—basic, mundane, even sometimes undelightful things—and have the best time doing them. He's funny and I'm goofy and together, we'd have a funny, goofy time.

> Honoring his lovable traits can **free you to trust your judgment** even more deeply.

He was thoughtful. Once I mentioned in passing that I wanted to try this new lip color I saw in an issue of *Essence*. He worked security at a Rite Aid at the time and called me at home one evening to ask me to come outside. He'd found the lipstick and surprised me with it. It was a small but heart-touching gesture.

He was a fantastic listener. I could tell him the most arbitrary, why-the-heck-am-I-even-saying-this-out-loud story and he'd not only listen but engage. Ask questions. Sometimes follow up about it a few days later. Something special happens inside when I know someone is really listening to the minutia spilling out of my scattered mind. It makes me feel loved.

Your used-to-be gave you an opportunity to see, in action, qualities you appreciate in a partner. Honoring his lovable traits can free you to trust your judgment even more deeply. Maybe he was a great provider, or a really generous and concerned citizen of the world, or a hustler with a by-any-means spirit. Take all of those great things about him and declare to God: This is what I want, but better. Ask him to enhance them. Magnify them. Make the things that worked even greater and the things that didn't work more complementary to your needs and personality.

Teedra Moses is every kind of fierce and her music holds a mirror up to the thoughts and sentiments of women. In "Rescue Me," she sings with confidence that one day, the man she's waiting for will find her. Because Teedra believes and sang so, I can believe and hopefully, you can hold on to your faith too. Your king may be taking the slow walk through the longest labyrinth of time but when he shows up, trust he'll be equipped with the characteristics you hold near and dear and some bonus qualities that will make him not just a man, but the man.—*J.H.D.*

Affirmation: *God knows what I like but more important, he knows what I need.*

Reflection: What were your exes' extraordinary qualities? Make a list of the good things about not only your most recent used-to-be, but other exes and people you generally admire in your life. Use it to create clarity about the qualities that are most important and valuable to you in a partner.

Keisha's Outro

Healing was not easy or quick. The pressure to get over the breakup hung over me like a heavy rain cloud when you don't have an umbrella. I tried to push myself and hurry to feel better rather than sit in the pain. I found myself agonizing over the length of time it was taking me to bounce back from this breakup. I compared my healing journey to others. I bemoaned the thought of how he had moved on while I was still brokenhearted.

Eventually, I chose to worry less about the time it was taking to be healed and just embraced the process of healing—the up days and the down days, the questioning days, the fearful days, and the hopeful days. Healing is a personal journey. It also isn't linear. It's less about dates on a calendar and more about what any given day brings you. Your healing can't be compared to someone else's or even your journey in a previous relationship. This time around, it took longer to work through my feelings of sadness and betrayal.

The most painful part was accepting that my love journey was open-ended. I didn't know what was next. And I had to do all of this while watching friends and family having kids and celebrating with them, not knowing when or if I had that in my future. The dashed dreams and unknown journey ahead hurt just as much as the breakup itself.

Mary J. Blige, the Queen of Breakup Songs, said it in "Whole Damn Year." It has taken a whole year to try to fully put this heartbreak behind me. I'm still learning to trust myself and trust someone else in my space. This heartbreak snatched my usual lighthearted, hopeful innocence, and it hasn't been easy to get it back. But there's a glimmer of a hopeful romantic fighting her way back up inside of me. She's not dead yet, she's just not as loud as she can be.

> **Don't put yourself** on a must-be-healed timetable.

Healing took work. The laborious process of digging into each emotion for this devotional and seeking God through my spiritual practices, the power of music, and the passing of time all were part of that work. Tears have now been replaced with smiles and laughter. I no longer have to stop myself from crying when I share stories about good times I had with him. I share them with laughter or joy for what they meant in the moment. I also no longer get furious when I remember the bad times.

The best advice I have for you as I come to the end of my healing process is to be kind to yourself while you go through the stages of heartbreak. Don't put yourself on a must-be-healed timetable. And don't forget to check in with yourself along the way. A journaling practice is one of the best ways to nurture yourself through your healing journey. It creates a consistent opportunity to identify where you are emotionally and remind yourself where you're going.

This 60-day devotional may be longer or shorter than you need. Wherever you find yourself on that spectrum, it's okay. You'll come out better for putting in the work to be whole. You'll rise again like a phoenix and on your best day, I hope you run into your ex when you're looking fabulous and able to smile—and realize that you're not the one who lost!

Janelle's Outro

I wasn't my usual random song-singing, spontaneous dance-moving, cheesy joke-cracking self for a long, long time. I still had joy, but a more dominant helplessness made it effete and unable to radiate with its typical vibrancy. Then, following a day that was nothing particularly special, my spirit forgot to be sad and let slip a few lines of an Earth, Wind & Fire classic while I was in the shower. It felt good, so I did it again. There have been times I've sobbed since then, others when I felt I was unlovable and undesirable, but the day I sang in the shower was the day I knew I was coming back. I was going to be all right.

Nothing is wrong with you.
Nothing is missing from you.

I have since decided I want to be free. It's a resolution to reclaim the inner peace and devil-may-care nature that were characteristically mine before fear and apprehension and what-ifs residually dammed my insides. Without noticing it, I'd been walking around injured, even before this heartbreak, and every broken relationship and dating failure intensified the severity of the last wound. Regular life stuff compounded that rejection, and I armored myself against more hurt by expecting mediocrity at best, tragedy at worst. Thousands of tears, hundreds of hours, dozens of tissues, and one healing heart later, I finally let it all go.

You know, barring homelessness, crippling injury, and death, I can think of three or four other suckish life events I'd rather endure than heartbreak. It is summarily the pits. You give up two, five, seven, however many months or years to a relationship and, when it doesn't end well, the fallout holds you emotionally captive for another two, five, seven or however many months or years until you get over it. The good news is when you bottom out, you're not doomed to stay there. God doesn't hold us hostage to our feelings, so when we're ready to come out, we can. God told us we have the power and thankfully, we do. We just have to activate it, believe in it, and honor it, regardless of the external noise around us.

> **God created you for an extraordinary purpose** and that's not to sit around being sad.

Nothing is wrong with you. Nothing is missing from you. I'm telling myself that at the same time I'm telling y'all. There is always room to elevate, grow, and be better, but the failure of a relationship doesn't equal your failure as a woman or a human. We're inundated with information trying to make itself relevant by showing us our faults and, if it hits us at the core at our most vulnerable times, it can infect us with the fear of not being enough. Not pretty enough. Not interesting enough. Not 'hood enough. Not bougie enough. Not smart enough. Not curvy enough. Not sexy enough. Never, ever let that become your truth. You are good, right now, as is, in this moment. You are good.

A few years ago, an engagement ring arbitrarily slid into my Pinterest feed. I don't know why, since all of my pins are about fashion, recipes, and DIY projects I'll never finish, but this ring was a gorgeous rose gold with a pear-shaped morganite center stone, vintage and contemporary cool at the same time. I'd never seen one like it before and I wanted to save it.

My brain was telling my arm to raise my hand to point my finger to touch the screen to press the button, but the sequence wouldn't work. Instead, fear overwhelmed me and I started crying. Hope can be terrifying and I cursed myself for even entertaining it. About an hour later, though, I went back, created a secret board called "The Maybe Board (With Fear of Hope)"—just a touch dramatic, I know—and pinned that ring along with two others and a picture of a guy I saw online who would make a pretty good prototype for the ring-giver.

I'm now married to a beautiful, brown-skinned man who enormously favors the guy I pinned on that Pinterest board. Just before I met him, I had "graduated" from therapy and settled into contentment being single. He's an alchemy of all the prayers prayed in this devotional and beyond, and he came to me with the intention to amplify the joy and wonder in my life. He does that regularly—I think we do it for each other—and he proposed with that very same ring I pinned with trembling fingers when I was still scared to open myself up to hope again.

We have literally journeyed together, y'all. You, me, and Keisha. I wrote these entries between helpless, boo-hoo sobs, emotionless indifference, and fire-hot anger when I couldn't type fast enough to get my fury out of my head. I'm no longer keeping a box of tissues stationed in every room of the house. I'm not crazy-texting anybody my heat in 6,000-character messages. It took me months to feel better than just okay, probably the longer part of a year, and I don't want to be back in that depth of relationship-related grief again. But I know if I ever am, God is there. I don't have to fight alone. Neither do you.

It can be hard to hear and digest good things about yourself when the devastation of a heartbreak makes it so easy to hyperfocus on your faults instead. I pray you sit in the totality of your gifts and blessings, knowing that God created you for an extraordinary purpose and that's not to sit around being sad. My song for this year was "Expect the Great" by Jonathan Nelson and I hope you do that—especially when it's scary, challenging, even unbelievable. I pray God meets you where you are in your faith walk and if he has to pick you up, I pray he does that too. And on the other side of this, I pray you experience the whimsical, spring-in-my-soul sensation of love again in a relationship worthy of you.

Acknowledgments

From Keisha

To my coauthor, homegirl, and bestest, Janelle. Thank you doesn't seem like it holds enough capacity for who you have been and continue to be in my life. I am grateful for our journey through heartbreak through all the stages, especially our tear-filled Chick-fil-A runs. Most of all, I am glad that you caught the vision to make what sucked into something that was a triumphant, in-your-face product to show our resilience.

I also truly am grateful for my family. They are my built-in cheerleaders. My mom, who is honest and will give me the truth, is an example of strength I can mirror, a believer in me who supports me in all my endeavors. I am grateful for you. To my little sister, Charlene, who is always rooting for me and will give me the "you're playing small" speech to gather me together, thank you for being you and loving me. I also must shout out the matriarch of my family, who prays consistently for me. Harriet Boyce is a force, and she's taught me to be my own force. I also have to put into print the love I feel for my niece, Aria. She is a little ball of love and joy and has been in tough times the light that shined brighter than darkness.

Thank you to my sister girls, especially Camille Williams, who has been my prayer partner and the voice God has used on many occasions to share the vision for my life. I appreciate you.

I have also been blessed to have the ancestors with me, my grandmother, Inez Jeffrey, and grandfather, Wilfred Jeffrey, cheering me on from the cloud of witnesses along with my sister, Makini.

From Janelle

I am the daughter of Marie, a woman who has modeled for me how beautiful love can be in a challenging time. She's sweet and kind with a kick of sass, and there's never been a moment I felt completely unloved in this or any other situation because Mommy was there being Mommy. I'm so thankful for you.

I am the granddaughter of Mildred and Wayman, who are forever my favorite married couple, and individually two of the most authentically good, gorgeous souls God created. I can do what I want to do because my mom and grandparents invested and believed in me all my life, and this devotional is a small thank-you to them for that freedom.

I am the mother of Skylar and Taytum, my amazing daughters, my heartthrobs and my smile-makers, and I am proud to have this book as tactile proof of tenacity to remind you of your capability to do your own hard things, things that take a long time, things that you can't figure how you can possibly make happen. I promise my best help to you, always.

I am the wife of Jerome, whose love, support, and cheerleading is an awesome, unending reward for all of the devastation and messiness I endured to get to our forever and ever amen. I had to belly-crawl through the mud to get to you, but our love and who we are because of it is the worthy prize.

I come from a village of awesome aunts—Aunt Virginia, Aunt Janet, Aunt Barbara, Aunt Florence—who have all listened to my life timeline of boyfriend horror stories and prayed and counseled me through with love, care, and uniquely individualized wisdom. I love y'all.

I am an only child but my friends are my sisters—Gretchen, Camille, Kimm, Cheresa, and Jamaica—who supported and prayed me through these broken hearts, of course, but who also have been a blessing to me not just in struggles and hardships but just by showing up as the delightful human beings they are.

Then there's Keisha: bestie, now coauthor. Thank you for pushing me through, pulling me up, cheering me on, and reining me in, and thank you for always being a person who puts action to your love and care. We are survivors of so many things, but I'm so thankful we've done the majority of that surviving together, and I'm even more grateful we got a chance to alchemize heartbreak into something good and useful, just like we said we would.

From Both of Us

Thank you, God. The ways that you show up to affirm, encourage, course-correct, and administrate can't be overstated or overlooked, and we are always in awe of and grateful to you. So, thank you, God.

We are thankful to Unity Books for seeing us. Not everyone recognized the value in a devotional about heartbreak but you did and we're grateful to you for selecting us. Double thanks to our Unity editor, Rev. Ellen Debenport, for your patience, insight, and gentle nudges to get and stay on track. We'll always appreciate how enthusiastic you've been about this project. It brought us joy to know that at least one other person caught our vision.

Our sincere thanks goes to the Unity staff for their dedication to producing such a beautiful product and to our talented homegirl Osayamen Asemota-Bartholomew of The Gift Agency LLC for her invaluable input around the book.

We love and thank our pastors, Rev. Dr. Kellie Hayes and Rev. Dr. Harold B. Hayes, Jr., for your prayers, advice, and encouragement through the years as we shook off rejections and setbacks. Your injections of faith allowed us to keep going. We're also grateful to our Hunter/Real Power AME family and our friends and accountability groupmates, Ericka and Candace, for their love, prayers, and celebration of our gifts. Ericka sent us an email about a Unity book publishing contest, we entered, and the rest is destiny.

We also want to acknowledge our readers, who are allowing us to journey with you through one of the most difficult and personal healing processes. We don't take that lightly. Please know we have already prayed for and are actively rooting for you, across these pages and beyond.

About the Authors

Rev. Tikeisha Harris, D.Min.

Rev. Tikeisha Harris, D.Min., isn't just a pastor. Her mission is to move past church walls and dive into the community where the real action is. A prolific speaker, writer, and public intellectual, her career in ministry spans print, podcasts, and pulpits. Tikeisha is a proud alumna of Lincoln University in Pennsylvania, the first HBCU, and she earned a master's in divinity from Wesley Theological Seminary and a doctorate in African-centered thought and ministry from McCormick Theological Seminary. She currently serves inspiration as interim pastor of New Liberation AME Church in Prince George's County, Maryland. Learn more about Tikeisha at *thsays.com*.

Janelle Harris Dixon

A writer since she won a dollar bill in an elementary school essay contest, Janelle Harris Dixon uses her platform as a journalist, storyteller, and editor to explore the experiences of women and her beloved Black folks. Her work has appeared in more than 40 publications including *Essence*, *The Washington Post*, and *Rolling Stone*, and her boutique editorial services agency, The Write or Die Chick, creates culturally competent content for a range of clients. She is a proud graduate of Lincoln University in Pennsylvania, the first HBCU, and lives on the ungentrified side of Washington, D.C. Follow Janelle at *thewriteordiechick.com*.

Headphones and Heartbreaks Playlist

Hear all the songs mentioned in this book!

go.unity.org/ heartbreakplaylist

SCAN ME